PRAISE FOR
BORN ON A ROTTEN DAY

"*Born On a Rotten Day* delivers the dirt on every sign and then some! A fun, fast-paced, and frantically funny read."

—Stuart Hazleton, author of *Sexscopes*

"A wry, clever look at the Darth Vader side of the zodiac."

—Trish McGregor, author of *Creative Stars: Using Astrology to Tap Your Muse*

"When you get to that place in your life when you're ready to hear the truth about yourself, read this book and laugh."

—Judith Turner, author of *The Hidden World of Birthdays*

"Hazel's insightful zingers perfectly describe every person who has ever pissed me off."

—Peter Bailey, webmaster/publisher of www.metamaze.com

"Hazel Dixon-Cooper has taken a perceptive, humorous look at the seamy underbelly of every sign. Her book is spot on for every sign . . . except for Sagittarius. We Sadges are perfect! Ha ha ha . . . [*burp*]!"

—Charlene Lichtenstein, author of *Herscopes*

Illuminating

and Coping with

the Dark Side

of the Zodiac

BORN

on a

ROTTEN

DAY

Hazel Dixon-Cooper

A Fireside Book
Published by Simon & Schuster
New York London Toronto Sydney

FIRESIDE
Rockefeller Center
1230 Avenue of the Americas
New York, NY 10020

For information about special discounts for bulk purchases,
please contact Simon & Schuster Special Sales:
1-800-456-6798 or business@simonandschuster.com

Designed by Diane Hobbing of SNAP-HAUS Graphics

Manufactured in the United States of America

20 19 18 17 16 15

Library of Congress Cataloging-in-Publication Data
Dixon-Cooper, Hazel.
    Born on a rotten day : illuminating the dark side of the zodiac / Hazel
Dixon-Cooper.
        p.   cm.
    1. Astrology. I. Title.

BF1711 .D55 2003
133.5—dc21   2002029660

ISBN-13: 978-0-7432-2562-5
ISBN-10:   0-7432-2562-7

Acknowledgments

Many people provided encouragement, expertise, and assistance during the process of writing this book. I gratefully thank them all, especially:

Margret McBride, my agent and bridge to the publishing world, for patiently answering all those first-time author questions; Marcela Landres, my remarkable and meticulous editor, whose friendly guidance and expert skill made the publishing experience painless; Larry Paquette, my dear friend, who helped burn the midnight oil and kept everything crossed; the Tuesdays, my writing family, who listened, critiqued, and supported me from first concept to finished product; Peter Bailey, my colleague, whose website, metamaze.com, saved me from hundreds of hours of research; my daughter, Wendy Cooper, who helped research this book; and my husband, Gary Cooper, who supported my dream.

For Bonnie Hearn Hill,
who taught me the value of Gemini time

Contents

BORN

ON A

ROTTEN

DAY

Chapter One

Malice in Wonderland

"I don't want to go among mad people," Alice remarked.
"Oh, you can't help that," said the Cat. "We're all mad here."

LEWIS CARROLL

Sign, Sign, Everywhere a Sign

Your Sagittarius boyfriend acts more like a loudmouthed circus clown than a happy-go-lucky charmer. Your Capricorn brother is a social-climbing snob. His Libra lover is shallow, fickle, and spends hours in front of the mirror.

You're confused or skeptical because none of the glowing descriptions in that $1.98 *Guide to the Zodiac* you thumbed through at the checkout counter match the neurotic bunch you live and work with in the real world.

The ancients believed that each of us contains a Universe. We are the center around which the vast threads and everyday minutiae of our life spins. Aries Rodney King asked, "Why can't we all just get along?" The honest question is, "Why can't you guys all get along with me?" Forget feel-good astrology and take a trip to the maladjusted side of the Universe. Outwardly, each of us may profess to live for others. Secretly, we all want what we want, right now.

Everyone is mad here, just as the Cheshire Cat said; and egotistical, obsessed, controlling, and moody. Knowing how each sign manifests those disagreeable qualities and learning how to control, aim, and fire the force of your own wicked twin within are the keys to staying ahead of that pack of monsters snapping at your heels.

The Basics

In astrology, there are four elements (Fire, Earth, Air, and Water), three qualities (Cardinal, Fixed, and Mutable), and two polarities (Masculine and Feminine).

FIRE signs are **selfish**. Aries, Leo, and Sagittarius are egotistical and demanding. This holier-than-thou bunch thinks the sun rises and sets on them. They attempt to control the rest of the world by force, intimidation, and temper tantrums. These human volcanoes erupt on a regular basis.

EARTH signs are **hardheaded**. Taurus, Virgo, and Capricorn are calculating, critical, and callous. They are preoccupied with work and penny-pinching and they point out everyone else's faults. Boring and churlish, they subscribe to the do-as-I-say-not-as-I-do philosophy of control. They dole out their affections as carefully as their money.

AIR signs are **flighty**. Gemini, Libra, and Aquarius are fickle, glib, and long-winded. They change lovers, jobs, and their minds as often as the rest of us change underwear. And with just as little thought. Rationalization and justification are Air's tools of control. They want us to think they are logical. In reality we usually give in just to shut them up.

WATER signs are **moody**. Cancer, Scorpio, and Pisces are the drama kings and queens. Self-destructive and manipulative, this awful bunch tries to control the rest of us through emotional blackmail. Water seeks not only its lowest level but yours as well. These characters will stop at nothing to find your weak spot and pick at it until you crack.

As for the qualities and polarities, the following comparisons will give you enough to get started.

Traditional astrology defines **Cardinal** as the initiator and leader. Rotten-truth translation: a bossy, pot-stirring meddler. Aries, Cancer, Capricorn, and Libra are the Cardinal signs.

The **Fixed** quality is defined as stable and persistent. Translation: a stubborn, exasperating bore. The Fixed signs are Aquarius, Leo, Scorpio, and Taurus. **Mutable** signs are described as flexible and adaptable. Translation: an inconsistent, self-delusional escapist. Gemini, Sagittarius, Pisces, and Virgo are the Mutable signs.

Finally, each sign is assigned a **Masculine** (outgoing) or **Feminine** (receptive) polarity. The rotten truth about this facet of the sun-sign personality is that masculine is an aggressor and feminine is an emotional manipulator.

Use the following tables as quick guides to the basic nature of each sign.

Traditional

Sign	Element	Quality	Polarity
Aries	Fire	Cardinal	Masculine
Taurus	Earth	Fixed	Feminine
Gemini	Air	Mutable	Masculine
Cancer	Water	Cardinal	Feminine
Leo	Fire	Fixed	Masculine
Virgo	Earth	Mutable	Feminine
Libra	Air	Cardinal	Masculine
Scorpio	Water	Fixed	Feminine
Sagittarius	Fire	Mutable	Masculine
Capricorn	Earth	Cardinal	Feminine
Aquarius	Air	Fixed	Masculine
Pisces	Water	Mutable	Feminine

Sign	Element	Quality	Polarity
Aries	Selfish	Bossy	Aggressive
Taurus	Hardheaded	Stubborn	Emotional Manipulator
Gemini	Flighty	Inconsistent	Aggressive
Cancer	Moody	Bossy	Emotional Manipulator
Leo	Selfish	Stubborn	Aggressive
Virgo	Hardheaded	Inconsistent	Emotional Manipulator
Libra	Flighty	Bossy	Aggressive
Scorpio	Moody	Stubborn	Emotional Manipulator
Sagittarius	Selfish	Inconsistent	Aggressive
Capricorn	Hardheaded	Bossy	Emotional Manipulator
Aquarius	Flighty	Stubborn	Aggressive
Pisces	Moody	Inconsistent	Emotional Manipulator

How does it work? Let's look at Aquarius. How can a person be flighty, stubborn, and aggressive? Water Bearers can change horses midstream. Question their decision, and you'll suffer a tiresome, in-your-face dissertation aimed at forcing your agreement. That's aggressive. They can have twenty lovers in a year. That's flighty. The fact that they are determined to keep going until they find true love and dumb enough to think it exists—that's stubborn.

Down the Rabbit-Hole

Now that you have the basics, it's time to take an in-depth look at the sun signs. Each sign has its own chapter, and each chapter is divided into the following subsections:

• **Approach with Caution.** Regardless of gender, age, or sexual preference, natives of the individual sun signs share some common bad behaviors.

• **If You Love One, Man or Woman.** Everyone's on their best behavior at the beginning of the love game. But before you decide to make it permanent, be warned. You could go to sleep with Betty Crocker and wake up with Lizzie Borden. Or fall for a character who color-codes your closet and tapes a lovemaking schedule on the bedroom door.

• **If You Are One—Born Rotten.** Yes, this is all about *you*. But, it's not all bad. Anyone reading it will soon discover that you are a force of nature not to be trifled with, in or out of the sack.

• **It's ALL Relative—The Family.** Ever wonder why your parents were so weird and your siblings so selfish, whiny, and mean? Find out here and also how to deal with that nutty bunch into which you did not ask to be born.

• **Office Party—Bitches, Snitches, and the Chronically Inert.** Life at the office. Who's the worst boss (none of them are good). Who's most likely to stab you in the back, or the front, on the scramble up the corporate ladder. How to handle churlish coworkers, cover your ass, and save your job.

• **Can't We All Get Along?** Tips for surviving the four worst behaviors of each sign (e.g., throw food to calm a Taurus and a brick to shut up an Aries).

• **Quick Tips for Emergencies.** A 911 list that may save your sanity, or at least buy you enough time to leave town.

• **A List of the Infamous and Ridiculous.** There's a little bit of each of them in each of us.

Enjoy your tour and remember, bad behavior isn't only in our genes—it's in our stars.

Chapter Two

Aries

March 21–April 19

Mommie Dearest Meets Peck's Bad Boy

Element: Fire. Aries is the dragon that lays waste to the countryside, then falls asleep, satisfied that it's burned a few small towns.

Quality: Cardinal. The only thing an Aries is qualified to lead is a chorus of kindergartners singing the Barney song.

Symbol: The Ram. Battering ram. Ram it to you. Butt-headed.

Ruler: Mars, the god of war and barroom brawls.

Favorite Pastime: Shooting first and asking questions later.

Favorite Book: The self-published *Journal of Personal Wisdom*.

Role Model: Yosemite Sam.

Dream Job: Sex therapist.

Key Phrase: "Are *you* talking to *me*?"

Body Part: The head, chronically aching from running into all those brick walls.

Approach with Caution

Aries, first sign of the zodiac, resides in the House of Self. Astrology textbooks describe the Ram as a charming, enthusiastic, natural-born leader who gleefully rushes through life with tremendous joie de vivre. The truth is, this bossy, egotistical motormouth is as self-absorbed as a two-year-old, and has a me-complex the size of Texas.

In Aries, Mars gives courage, determination, energy, passion, and ambition. He also bestows temperament, ego, and impulsive action. Just like Yosemite Sam, the typical Ram barrels through life daring anyone to cross his or her path. Be unlucky enough to get in the way, and you'll suffer a red-faced temper tantrum. Jumping up and down is optional. The worst thing you can do to an Aries is ignore them, the way you would ignore a cranky toddler who's in dire need of a nap.

Aries are reactive, not reasonable. By refusing to think before they act, Rams often ruin their chances for happiness by making wild assumptions without gathering all the facts. Being born without the humility gene has negated their ability to admit mistakes. Argue with one, and you'll suffer a barrage of irrational, angry shouting. Prove they are wrong, and they will react like that toddler who says, "Am not," then shrugs his baby shoulders and walks away.

If You Love One—Aries Man

Arrogant. Pompous. Vain. Cruel. Verbose. Show-off. I've been called all of these. Of course, I am.

HOWARD COSELL (MARCH 25)

Passionate, idealistic, and sentimental, the Aries man is part hero, part child, no matter what his age. He's as friendly as a puppy, downright fearless, and rather like one of those weighted clowns that children punch. You can knock him down, but he will always bounce back. And, for as long as he loves you, he will be faithful, sexy, and attentive. If you feel weak in the knees, make sure there's a sofa handy to fall on, because by the time you've swooned, this Romeo will have moved on to his next conquest.

Aries men are in love with love. The appeal is in the art of romance and the thrill of the chase, not your charming smile.

Some astrologers compare an Aries man to a knight in shining armor. However, you are just as likely to get run down by his charging steed as scooped up in a pair of loving arms. Sir Lancelot may have been bold and honest, but he was also a royal pain in the ass, all Aries traits. His ego ruined a kingdom when, in his eagerness to run his hand up Guinevere's dress, he conveniently forgot his vow to King Arthur. In Lance's point of view he was a hero, and to an Aries man, his point of view is the only one that counts.

The Ram fears mediocrity more than death. He would rather be the biggest jerk in town than just another anonymous working slob. He is subjective, bossy, and has a caustic wit he flings with careless abandon. He takes pride in being more self-centered than Scorpio and more obtuse than Taurus. He's sure he's right. Especially when he is wrong.

Male Rams come in two types. Bold, brash, and ready for action or shy, quiet, and ready for action. Don't be fooled by the shy type. He may come on all "Aw shucks" and toe shuffles, like Aries Dennis Quaid, but under that poker face, or enigmatic smile, his brain synapses are firing at 1,000 per minute, concentrating on the best way to get you into his bed in the shortest possible time.

On the door of the original Playboy Mansion in Chicago was a brass plate with the inscription *Si Non Oscillas, Noli Tintinnare—If you don't swing, don't ring.* Aries Hugh Hefner, the flip, hip, big daddy of hedonism, is still alive and well, and still the quintessential bad boy at seventy-six.

Remember all of this before you buy your wedding dress.

After the ceremony, he will expect you to worship the ground he makes you crawl on while he declares his need for freedom. He will require you to have the house sparkling, the grass mowed, and the cars washed, all before he gets home from his latest adventure. He'll leave a trail of dirty clothes from the front door to the shower, while shouting his dinner order over his shoulder.

When he appears at the table, he'll expect you to have a gourmet's delight in one hand and his favorite cold drink in the other. And, you'd better look like you just stepped out of the pages of *Vogue*. This man chases the ideal. He doesn't want a real woman, with real needs. He wants the adoration of Mommy and the ethereal qualities of a fairy princess, all wrapped up in the figure of a *Playboy* centerfold.

He thinks he is indestructible, but he's extremely accident-prone and seldom gets through life without a few broken bones, several concussions, and a couple of totaled cars. He is restless, fidgety, and has frequent headaches.

Just as he is either brash or shy, he'll either be a spendthrift or paranoid about starving to death. You'll have to clip coupons and buy pork and beans in bulk while he plays Mr. Fix-It with the plumbing. You'll learn to sew and to raise your own veggies while he attacks his latest moneymaking scheme with the same fierce energy that makes him shout at the TV and practice road rage in the church parking lot. If he's loose with cash, you'll have to work two jobs to keep the creditors off your back and a roof over your heads.

Mr. Ram communicates by temper tantrum. He will smash the glasses and put his fist through the wall one minute, then want to screw your brains out the next. And he will be genuinely surprised when you resist his ardor as you're bent over the dustpan, sweeping up shards of crystal.

Your favorite Martian will start a little war to have an excuse to slam out of the house and stay out until all hours. A Leo would announce that he's going out with the boys, and a Capricorn would tell you he's working late at the office, but

Aries needs to rationalize his bad behavior. If you're the bitch, then he is still the hero. The Greeks christened him the Ram. You can call him Butthead.

If You Love One—Aries Woman

I've been uncompromising, peppery, intractable, monomaniacal, tactless, volatile, and oft times disagreeable.

Bette Davis (April 5)

She is independent, fun loving, and honest. She's not a game player or easily shocked. This lady can clean her own house, balance her own checkbook, and put the pieces of a shattered dream back together with such aplomb that no one's the wiser. She loves romance, sentiment, and men who are bold. And her ardor will not fade over the years. Just a minute, bud. Before you jump in that long line of frantic, scrambling men, take note. Those haggard guys are looking for the nearest exit.

If it doesn't begin with "I" and end with "me," the female Aries isn't interested in the conversation. Ask how her day has been and be prepared for all the boring details. She thinks that because she's fascinated with herself, why, naturally, so are you.

A female Ram will compete with you on every level. Land a huge account, and she'll tell you that it was just dumb luck, while touting her own conquest of the day. Tell her you just won the Lotto and she'll say, "That's nice, but I just broke a fingernail!"

She's impatient, critical, and will start and stop as many projects as a Gemini. The difference is that when Aries starts something, it's with one intent only, to end up at the head of the line. There's nothing altruistic about this babe. She wants power, status, and lots of dough. And, to get it, she'll drive herself, and you, to frenzy. If you want to be treated like a man, marry any other sign in the Universe. If you want to be told what to wear, eat, think, plus be constantly reminded that she is faster, better, and smarter than you, here's your girl. Think of Mama Rose in *Gypsy,* the eternal stage mother, the woman who expects everyone to live her dream, dangle in her shadow.

She's as jealous as Scorpio. But, don't mistake her green-eyed snarling as insecurity. Jealousy in all Rams comes from the need to be first. Even the kids will have to take a backseat to her in your affections. Prone to frequent temper tantrums, she is the perfect example of a pushy broad determined to get her way come hell or high water. She's not squeamish about who she has to walk on, or sleep with, to get to the top of her chosen field.

Joan Crawford and archrival Bette Davis are perfect examples of why the Aries female is known as the Queen Bitch of the Universe, and deserves the title. The legendary feud between the two stars was well known in the Hollywood of the forties and fifties.

Davis said of Crawford, "She's slept with every male star at MGM except Lassie." In return Crawford said, "I don't hate Bette Davis . . . take away the pop eyes, the cigarette, and those funny clipped words and what have you got?"

When the pair co-starred in *Whatever Happened to Baby Jane,* Bette had a Coca-Cola machine installed to irk Joan because of her affiliation with Pepsi. Joan got revenge by putting weights in her pockets when Davis had to drag her across the floor during a key scene. In an interview after filming wrapped, Davis said, "The best time I had working with Joan was when I pushed her down the stairs."

Remember this with your own firebrand. For every night you snuggle with her on the sofa, you'll spend the next ten either dodging verbal or physical darts, or in an endless whirl of friends, dinners out, and rushing to be the first in line at the latest movie.

The female Ram can outgun, outrun, outshoot, outtalk, and

outsmart everyone around her. How do you know? Just ask her. Like a Leo man, an Aries woman is a legend—in her own mind.

If You Are One—Born Rotten

It's not the earth the meek inherit; it's the dirt.

From CAMELOT

You are capable of soaring to any height. Sometimes by utilizing your determined Martian energy. Sometimes by hopping on the nearest broom. You play all the angles, are jealous, competitive, and totally oblivious to your own worst behavior.

You don't do laid back. Instead, you picture yourself as The Great Enlightener and spend your time haranguing the rest of us into submission. You are nearly as tactless as a Sagittarius stuffing his size-twelve foot in his mouth. At the least, you have a gift of gab that can make a Gemini cry, and at your worst, your bellicose attitude loses friends and starts family arguments.

Since your favorite topic of conversation is the endless minutiae of your personal existence, you are also a colossal bore. Of course this means little or nothing to you as long as you get to hear yourself talk. You are genuinely perplexed when rooms empty at your appearance and all your friends get Caller ID, then refuse to answer the phone.

Your home is a combination trophy shop and arsenal. The wall next to the gun cabinet is filled with heads from your latest Bambi-shoot. The table in the corner holds a high school debate team cup and a marathon dance blue ribbon. Pictures of relatives line the hallways and the basement is stuffed with assorted military gear, World War II surplus K-rations, and bottled water.

From the time you learned about the birds and bees (and

people would be surprised at how early an age that was) until you're dead, sex is the uppermost thought in your mind. In grammar school, you played doctor. As a teen, you wore out the backseat of the family sedan. And as an adult, you forever fall in and out of love.

When you aren't filing your fingernails, you are sharpening your rapier wit on unfortunate friends or instigating family feuds. Actually, the word *friend* is something of a misnomer, because you usually choose people as friends in direct proportion to how they can help further your own plots and plans.

You Martians climb the social ladder as eagerly as Capricorns, but with far less finesse. You'll transparently kiss up to the most powerful person around and have the nerve not to blush with shame when you are accused of that very thing. In fact, you'll twinkle and smile, be all the more charming, and get away with the whole mess.

Aries is the sign of the sculptor, warmonger, Chippendale dancer, and the bad half of a good-cop-bad-cop team. Rams are also great athletes, freedom fighters, and bank robbers (e.g., Aries Clyde Barrow).

You were the type of child that flung open the closet door and dared any monster living there to get out of your space. You also had to get burned before you believed that the stove was really hot. You still do. And therein lies your strength. You have no shame, and more nerve than a one-legged wirewalker.

You have a true warrior spirit and are relentless when fighting for a cause, or a person in whom you believe. Once you learn to truly listen to other viewpoints, and accept that you are not always right, the rest of the Universe will fall at your feet. However, in battle no other sign can match you.

Scorpio may try to sting, but a well-aimed barb flung straight from your flaming tongue singes the Scorpion's tail. Cancer and Pisces cringe and fade away with a single, smoldering look. Taurus, Virgo, and Capricorn soon learn what

Scorched Earth Policy means when they try to rage at, nag, or trample you. Your ability to push Air signs Gemini and Aquarius into the ozone with your one-upmanship soon bursts their respective bubbles. And you have wishy-washy Libra begging for mercy when you demand that he make a decision—now! You and the other Fire signs, Leo and Sagittarius, understand each other on a soul level, and therefore rarely have serious confrontations.

Your philosophy is, "Nothing ventured, nothing gained." You couldn't care less what others think. You are a supremely confident, rugged individualist who lives life on your own terms. Let the rest of the world bake cookies and tend their gardens. Years from now, when all those folks you've left in the dust are weeding the window boxes at the old people's home, you can give them the giant raspberry as you race by in your Drop-Dead Red, supercharged hot rod.

It's ALL Relative—The Aries Family

"Anything You Can Do, I Can Do Better"

Song title

An Aries-ruled household is a curious mixture of flophouse and twenty-four-hour truck stop. The telephone rings constantly, assorted characters come and go at odd hours. Animals roam through the open doors, and loud music blares over the TV, which blares over the laughter, arguing, and cheering. Here is the home where the fun and mayhem never stop.

The Aries family records life in minute detail. Your parents will have a video of you from the first ultrasound to the last push, and will frequently invite the neighbors over to watch the show.

Classic movie buffs will remember *You Can't Take It with You*, a great tale of a wonderfully eccentric family, all a little nutty and all, in typical Ram fashion, so preoccupied with their individual desires that they nearly lost everything. Grandfather was the thrifty, quiet Ram who squirreled away enough money to fend off the biggest bank in town just in the nick of time.

To be sure, the arguments can turn ugly, and the fights between your shrewish Aries mom and belligerent dad Ram will make you crawl under the bed to avoid the flying missiles. But, while the fireworks are furious, they seldom last long. Five minutes later the folks are snuggling on the couch wondering why you aren't sitting there watching *L.A. Law* with them. Aries family disruptions are like the ripples in a pond. Trouble is, in this household, someone is always tossing in a rock.

An Aries parent will have the last word if it kills both of you, and no matter what you did, or how big a medal you got for the accomplishment, he or she will point out at least one thing you could have done better. Or worse, tell you how they *did* do it better.

Your Aries mother will expect you to live up to her standards of what she thinks your life should be, which are not necessarily the ones she's set by example. Ram dads often try to wrestle their two-hundred-pound sons to the ground, just to prove they are still number one. Your Aries father will work hard for the family, and won't be stingy with any money he has jingling in his pocket at the end of the day. Unfortunately, there's not much left after dear old Dad makes the rounds of the sporting goods store and the hobby shop, then drops by the newsstand for the latest copy of *Playboy*. It's not that he doesn't love you, kid, it's just that he comes first.

However, your Aries parents will also cheer the loudest, fight for you the hardest, and brag about you until the neighbors lock their doors.

Aries infants are the most demanding in the Universe. Your Aries darling is born with a will as strong as yours, and an impervious attitude toward discipline. You say, "Don't touch that," and baby immediately grabs the object in question and stands there with a big smile, looking you straight in the eye. You say, "Children should be seen and not heard," and your little sweetheart marches into the center of the room shrieking. From the moment of birth, you'll need track shoes, the patience of Job, and a very big stick.

Aries siblings compete for everything. As babies, they grab the toy you just picked up and the candy out of your hand. As teens, they are merciless teasers. They will borrow your clothes, money, and car without asking and never apologize for tearing your best dress, crumpling a fender, or neglecting to pay back the piggy bank. It would be a good idea to install a lock on your bedroom door and wear the only key on a chain around your neck.

It will never be quiet, but your Mars-ruled home will also never be dull. Besides, having Aries parents practically guarantees that you'll be the first in your class to have your own car. You could do a lot worse. So learn to smile, nod, and tune out. Better yet, buy yourself a set of earplugs.

Office Party—Bitches, Snitches, and the Chronically Inert

I consider myself influential, as opposed to manipulative.
RICHARD HATCH (APRIL 8), *SURVIVOR* 2000

Whether dynamo or dud, the Aries boss thinks he or she was born to lead. This is the glad-handing, quick-tempered, finger-in-every-pie, eye-on-every-desk management type.

Boss Ram is a workaholic superachiever who keeps a change of clothing in the executive washroom and a sofa in her office in case she decides to pull an all-nighter—either drafting her latest corporate raider plan, or with the new junior manager in marketing. She will drive you and the rest of your sweating coworkers with all the zeal of a missionary baptizing heathens until your department is first to turn in its monthly reports, or your division is first in sales. *First* is the keyword. Everything is a competition to Aries, and your boss never takes her eyes off the finish line.

You will always know where you stand with the Ram. He makes the rules. You obey. He develops strategy. You carry it out. He has boundless energy and enthusiasm. Unless you do too, you'd better keep a jar of vitamins in your desk and the coffee pot on high. Let him catch you yawning, or bitching about being overworked, and he will fix it so you have plenty of time to rest and reflect in the unemployment line.

Be careful of asking Aries coworkers that casual question "How are you today?" You are liable to hear the answer in excruciating detail. And don't bother to tell them how your day has been. They couldn't care less.

The moment your Aries coworker decides he, or she, wants your job, you will have an Olympic-size competition on your hands. First, it will be a contest to see who can turn in the most reports, ask for more work, crunch the most numbers. If, by some miracle, you manage to keep a step ahead, the Ram will start sneaking behind your back to discredit you. Aries can play the two-face game, almost as well as Pisces, but for a very different reason. Aries must win. It's a compulsion. You will become The Enemy, whether or not you deserve the title. It feeds their overactive egos, justifies their bad behavior, and eases the guilt (like the kid caught at the cookie jar) they nearly always feel.

To survive, keep telling them, "You are the greatest." Verbally pat their heads often and say things like, "I couldn't have done this without you." Don't worry too much. It's easy to trip up one who's trying to steal your job. Rams sneak the same way a little kid does—noisily. You'll catch on to them in about five minutes because they've told so many people what they are up to that you've already been warned.

Irk them by bragging that the boss told you that she couldn't survive the rat race without you at her side. Gaslight them by patronizing their childish egos and ignoring the constant deluge of family pictures they e-mail.

Can't We All Get Along?

Short of committing an act of violence, how in the world can you control an Aries and keep your wits? Here's some advice on dealing with these irascible hotheads.

Ram Egos

A Ram may be as demanding as a toddler climbing on your lap, but he or she is also nearly as vulnerable. Both sexes have a fragile self-image and need generous amounts of praise and attention. When your Ram comes home with bruised feelings and a battered ego from being the world's most misunderstood human, turn on the fireplace, open the wine, and snuggle down for a heart-to-heart talk. Soon you both will be smiling.

Headstrong Rams

Aries is the most impatient sign in the zodiac. However, if you take time to observe them, you'll understand that it is usually a self-directed intolerance. Rams are born with a overpowering urge to be first, a keen knowledge that they are not, and a very low tolerance for stress. Like their metaphorical symbol, your human Ram takes the shortest route to achieve a goal, even if it means a blind leap of faith. This results in frequent frustration, lost tempers, and a tremendous amount of guilt over the simplest mistake. Keep yours from self-destructing by helping them redirect their energy into something physical and positive, like painting the porch or scrubbing the bathroom.

Motormouth Rams

Aries chatter constantly. They truly think you must value their opinion, otherwise you wouldn't be sitting there listening. You could throw a brick to shut yours up. But, you would just end up nursing them back to health because they were too busy talking to duck. Rams do have a sense of fair play, and once yours gets the rules straight, you'll be able to carry on, if not an equal, at least a tolerable two-sided conversation. They appreciate honesty, so be direct, but kind. Tell your Ram that you appreciate his opinions, but it's important that he listen without interruption until you've finished talking. Providing a bowl of popcorn he can munch while you talk helps.

Domineering Rams

Rams believe they were born to lead, so it's pretty much futile to try to boss one around. When you want something, you need to use reverse psychology, and toss in a bit of a challenge for good measure.

Example: Your Aries was supposed to replant the flowerbeds before the family reunion next Sunday. Demanding that she finish the job she started three months ago will only push her peevish button. Instead, lavishly praise what she's already accomplished, then suggest that perhaps you should call a professional. Tell her you understand she can't do everything, and besides, a real gardener knows more than anyone about shrubs and flowers. For good measure, casually mention you saw that the neighbor she detests (there's always someone a Ram detests) has nearly finished planting her new rose hedge.

Before you can thumb through the Yellow Pages, your Ram will have raced out the door headed for the nursery. And, before the week is out, you'll have the prettiest garden in town.

Quick Tips for Emergencies
- ϒ Rams need lots of attention and frequent praise.
- ϒ Remember their egos are as fragile as a toddler's and act accordingly.
- ϒ Reverse psychology is key to getting your way.
- ϒ Physical exercise quells a temper tantrum.
- ϒ Gaslight them by ignoring or patronizing them.

Hot-headed Rams
Attila the Hun
Otto von Bismarck
John Wayne Bobbitt
Lucretia Borgia
Casanova
Butch Cassidy
Robert Downey, Jr.
Rodney King
Captain James T. Kirk (and William Shatner)
Scarlett O'Hara

Chapter Three

Taurus

April 20–May 20

What's Mine Is Mine, What's Yours Is Mine

Element: Earth. Taurus Earth is like a swamp filled with ancient trees covered in moss. Maneuvering through this bog feels like a dream in which you try to walk but get nowhere.

Quality: Fixed. Taurus is the original immovable object.

Symbol: The Bull. Bullish. Bullheaded. Raging bull. Full of bull.

Ruler: Venus, the goddess of lust, jealousy, and hedonism.

Favorite Pastime: Passing judgments over dinner.

Favorite Book: *The Gluttonous Gourmet.*

Role Model: Uncle Scrooge.

Dream Job: Hanging judge.

Key Phrase: "Why do you make me hit you?"

Body Part: The throat, usually sore from bellowing.

Approach with Caution

Taurus, the second sign of the zodiac, resides in the House of Money and Possessions. Traditional astrology kindly describes this Fixed-Earth sign as a steadfast, discriminating, thrifty homebody who is a great cook. Your real-life version more closely resembles a stubborn, judgmental, boring miser with a weight problem.

Mention Taurus, and most people conjure up a mental image of Sagittarius Munroe Leaf's Ferdinand the Bull, peacefully chewing sweet grass and batting his big, bovine eyes in placid contentment. Lean across the fence and he'll let you scratch behind his ears. Climb over that fence and attempt to pick a few of the daisies growing in his pasture, and you'll soon discover the dark side of tranquillity—Raging Bull. With practice, you can spot an imminent charge. His or her face darkens visibly as the temper rises. The eyes veil, the jaw juts, or sets, ever so slightly. Some unconsciously lower the head a bit and look up at you as a real bull does before it charges. Depending on how self-controlled yours is, you have from one second to a few minutes to brace yourself.

Venus rules Taurus and here, this ancient bad girl bestows an insatiable appetite. Bulls can never get enough approval, possessions, food, rest, or sex.

Bulls are emotional, not intellectual. Relying on instinct rather than fact, they often fall victim to their own judgmental natures. Being born without the seeing-another-person's-point-of-view gene has voided all reason and logic. Arguing your case will only enrage them and craze you. Prove your point, and Taurus will simply blink those big, soulful eyes and look at you as if you were speaking a foreign language.

If You Love One—Taurus Man

The great question—which I have not been able to answer—is "What does a woman want?"

Sigmund Freud (May 6)

He's patient, prudent, and persevering, a tower of strength on whom you can lean. You'll fall for his shy charm and those big, sad eyes. He may remind you of a slow-talkin', slow-walkin' hero like Gary Cooper or Henry Fonda. His needs are simple: home and hearth, a good woman, and a nest egg for that rainy day. Before you start drooling, read on, sweetie.

Taurus may offer old-shoe comfort, but what you're likely to get is an army-boot mentality. Hook up with the Bull and either do things his way, or do your thing alone. He won't mind your independence, if it benefits him in some way, and as long as dinner is ready when he appears.

Don't expect to be showered with praise and lavish attention. Do expect to be cast into the role of the little woman. Of all the men in the Universe, this one expects the 1950s textbook version. He will buy your clothes, pick your friends, and criticize your beliefs. He is judgmental and fixed in his ideas, attitudes, and prejudices. Nothing you can say or do will change him. You'll have the distinct feeling of being boiled alive slowly, just as the proverbial frog, and you will be right. Mr. T invented the smothering relationship.

He is jealous, possessive, and obsessive. Piss him off and he'll hold a grudge. Unfortunately, it's not a silent one. He will snipe and pick and make nasty remarks until you want to bash his head with the nearest blunt object.

William Randolph Hearst provides a classic example of the Taurean love of possessions gone berserk. He spent tens of millions of dollars to build himself a real castle filled with priceless art and furnishings from all over the world. According to Hollywood legend, Hearst built the castle for his ladylove,

Marion Davies, because his wife refused to divorce him. Talk about a gilded cage and a grim fairy tale. You would think a guy with all that power and dough would have no trouble buying off a wife. Well, Marion didn't get a wedding ring and she didn't get the castle. It was his castle, filled with his possessions. She was just a living adornment for the furniture.

The Taurean love for food is renowned, and the Bull likes to eat. By your second anniversary he could be wearing triple-X sweats and a truss. He is capable of eating himself into multiple heart attacks and will expect you to play nurse for real.

His idea of excitement is switching from the food channel to *Wrestlemania*. It's convenient, not too far from the refrigerator, and best of all, doesn't cost anything. You may be irresistible, and he may love you madly, but he will never understand why you need any other company but his. If he does take you out, it will be to one of his favorite restaurants, where he'll be too busy stuffing his face to make decent conversation.

He's a cheapskate. Only a Taurus could live on a beer-and-beans budget unnecessarily. He may have millions, but you'll never see the bank accounts, although you might get an allowance. If you do get his money, it will only be because you outlived him, or murdered him in his sleep. The latter will become a tempting idea as time goes by.

Sigmund Freud's use of psychoanalysis was a breakthrough in the field of psychiatry. But only a Taurus man could be at once so obtuse and so egotistical as to define a woman's frustrations and unresolved emotional distress as penis envy. Freud's Scorpio ascendant only fueled his obsession with sex. Virtually all of his theories held sex responsible for all the emotional ills of mankind. Including Sigi, who had a lengthy affair with his wife's younger sister. The original Freudian slip.

The Bull's favorite game is Grand Inquisitor. He will expect you to report every detail of your day. He will also rummage through your private papers and read your diary at the first opportunity. If you have a past and are foolish enough to reveal it, he is capable of using it against you at any time for the rest of your life. Your best bet is a safe–deposit box, and to lie your ass off.

He is so stable, he's inert. Work and home are all he knows, or needs. Although he's marathon man between the sheets, what he really wants is a housekeeper, and is so insensitive that you must hit him with a skillet to get attention. If you're the type who needs excitement now and then, you could lick the light socket or have an affair. With a Taurus man, I'd opt for the former. The Bull is not the forgive-and-forget type. Although he hates change, he is perfectly capable of tossing you out on your ear one day and moving in your replacement the next.

If You Love One—Taurus Woman

The trouble with some women is that they get all excited about nothing, then marry him.

Cher (May 20)

She is Mother Earth in a black teddy. She is faithful, courageous, and strong. The Taurus woman seeks security and a dependable mate. Money is not important as long as you can provide a nice home and the basic necessities. She has a refreshingly simple viewpoint of life. Picture fresh-baked bread, a cozy love nest, and her dainty hand in yours. Before you fall on your knees to offer that engagement ring, picture an iron hand in that little velvet glove.

She's as tough as nails, no matter how hard she tries to convince you, and herself, otherwise. She is also a victim. You, on the other hand, will be a bastard from the instant you slip the wedding ring on her finger. Don't forget it.

If you argue, beware; she has all the wrath of her male counterpart and the same penchant for violence. Without hesitation, she will throw whatever she happens to have in her hand, including a butcher knife, at your head.

Food is an emotional pleasure. She will eat when she's happy, depressed, angry, or just plain hungry, which is most of the time. By your second anniversary, her summer wardrobe will consist of an oversize blue muumuu and flip-flops. In winter the muumuu will be red and she'll replace the sandals with hunting socks. She'll pull the whole outfit together with a woolen shawl she found at the secondhand store. Along with the weight gain will come a natural slowing down of the urge to keep the house tidy. Her reasoning will be that it only gets dirty again. She will, however, expect you to work two jobs to pay for her new car. She deserves it for putting up with you.

She likes to start family feuds, then sit back and observe the mayhem. Emotionally as sensitive as a drill sergeant, she spouts orders, makes pronouncements, plans everyone's future, and expects blind obedience. Try to reason with her, and she'll set her jaw and plant her swollen feet.

A female Taurus doesn't believe in anything she can't clutch in her greedy little hands. Possessing an idea, other than where her next meal is coming from, is as foreign to this lady as is the thought of you with another woman. Get caught with your pants down and she may refuse to believe her own eyes. Security, even with a lowlife, is more important than her self-esteem.

She's easily depressed. Running out of vanilla ice cream can cause a funk. When down, she resembles the maniacal nurse in *Misery*. Yours may not be your greatest fan, but she's certainly capable of hobbling you to keep you home. Not physically, but emotionally and financially. She will spend your money faster than you can earn it, while investing hers in an account you'll never find.

She is a martyr. She blames the world, her job, the kids, and you for her own faults. If she has four plates of lasagna, then is ill later, it's your fault for letting her eat so much. If she runs over a cat on the way to work, it's the cat's fault for being in the road.

She is also a survivor. Consider Russia's Catherine the Great. Her family was duped into allowing an arranged marriage with the heir to the throne of Russia. When the prince turned out to be a half-wit, and Russia, a near-barbaric country, Catherine's mother protested the travesty and was dispatched back home without a good-bye. Catherine was nineteen.

Kate the Great not only survived; she thrived. She used her earthy sensuality to screw her way into the hearts of the prince's personal guard and soon produced a bouncy, and normal, baby boy. Rumor had it that the baby's father was a Cossack guard. Didn't matter to a people who had been subjected to the whims of a madman. Later, with another lover's help, Catherine seized power, had the evil emperor dispatched, and saved the country. She ruled for nearly forty years.

Your lady bull is much less likely to kill you to get revenge, but she will get it, just the same. She won't use emotional blackmail, as a Water sign would, or come at you screeching like a Fire sign. She prefers the role of judge and jury and to exact her punishment for the rest of your life.

When you're ready to dump her, and who could blame you, make all your preparations in secret and take a day off work to move without her knowledge. Sounds cruel, but it could save you a trip to the hospital, or the morgue. If you behave so consistently bad that she throws you out, just toss your toothbrush and one change of underwear in a paper sack and hit the road. She will keep everything else. Unfortunately, for her, it takes a lot to make a Taurus kick you out. She is the original ball and chain. Make her cry, and she will lie on the couch sucking up the Häagen-Dazs all day. Make her mad, and you'll lie on the floor, nursing a black eye.

If You Are One—Born Rotten

Rule #1: I'm never wrong. Rule #2: When in doubt, refer to Rule #1.

Anonymous

You are stubborn, inflexible, and so laid back you're in a coma. That's on a good day. As with all true forces of nature, there's nothing subtle about you. You're capable of wrath measuring ten on the Richter scale. In your heart, you believe you are right, even when you are proven wrong, and are so narrow-minded that you can get stuck in a rut so deep you need a ladder to climb out. That's OK with you because you think it's a safe and sane way to live.

You are perfectly willing to plod through life without trampling anyone's toes, as long as everyone understands you are boss. However, you will deliberately shake up things at home in a spot check to see who's really on your side. You need constant adoration from your spouse, demand blind obedience from your children, and will bust a skull now and then to assure it. You forget your angry outbursts as soon as they erupt, and can't understand why the relative you laid low an hour ago won't share the nice dinner you've just cooked.

In romance you have the approach of a dentist's drill. You can knock anybody's socks off, but after the deed, there's no glow. You are snoring before your partner stops breathing hard. You wake up in a few minutes, ready to rock and roll. By then your partner is sleepy. Of course, this means little or nothing to you as long as you get your jollies again.

Cleaning house means clearing away last month's pile of empty pizza boxes and potato chip bags. You are a junk-food junkie. Your favorite clothes are cheesy sweats to slug around in at home.

You are often underestimated because of your calm surface temperament, and you have hidden talents you seldom use.

Taurus is the sign of the writer, artist, dictator, district attorney, and hanging judge.

That obtuse Taurean nature you're famous for is a ruse. You understand. You just don't care what others think and have no use for anyone who doesn't measure up to your personal value system. You won't be swayed from a course of action and your strength lies in the fact that you don't need anyone's approval but your own.

You are one of the zodiac's true homebodies. You are not flighty, or flirty, or empty-headed. You are capable, thrifty, and cagey. You understand instinctively your powerful nature and aren't afraid to use it to further yourself in life, but you need to learn that your glare and occasional snort is enough to make most people take a step back. Control your famous rampages, choose your battles carefully, and nothing can stop you.

Lower your head, roll back those eyeballs, and the Water signs of Pisces and Cancer will wilt. A Scorpio may incite a rage, but even they are no match for your raw anger. Fire signs Aries, Leo, and Sagittarius belch brimstone and lava, but your earthy nature keeps renewing itself long after they've been reduced to smoking ash heaps. Gemini, Libra, and Aquarius, the airhead bunch, cause only buzzing noises in your ears as they try to figure you out. A flick of your tail dispatches these characters. You and fellow Earth signs Virgo and Capricorn understand each other on a soul level, and therefore, rarely have serious confrontations.

Your philosophy is, "A penny saved is a penny earned." You couldn't care less about expounding on the mysteries of the Universe. Let everyone else whirl and gyrate, foam at the mouth, and faint. You are too busy earning your first million. Years from now when your ex-lovers and other enemies are sitting on the lawn at the old people's home, you can give them the one-fingered wave as you pass by in your chauffeured limousine.

It's All Relative—The Taurus Family

> *Bilbo's cousins the Sackville-Bagginses were, in fact, busy measuring his rooms . . . Bilbo was "presumed dead," and not everybody that said so was sorry to find the presumption wrong.*
>
> THE HOBBIT

A Taurus-ruled home reminds me of one of those film noir movies of the 1950s. Assorted treacherous relatives live in a stately mansion at the mercy of their rich-but-miserly-and-manipulating mother or father. Lionel Barrymore in real life.

Your Taurus parents will quiz you after dates, search your room regularly, and tell you what you're going to be when you grow up. Don't worry, kid. It's a no-win situation. If you become what they want you to be and are unhappy, they'll conveniently forget they pushed so hard. If you have a mind of your own and use it, they'll snort and blow and threaten to kick your butt out. Just leave when you're ready. The old man will be too interested in the ball game to get off the couch and track you down. And Ma will be too busy stuffing her face in consolation. They will refuse to send money. They wouldn't have, anyway. Taurus parents cling to their possessions until they're dead.

A few years ago speculation swirled as to whether or not Queen Elizabeth II would abdicate the throne to Prince Charles. The reason she didn't was attributed to his scandalous love triangle that embarrassed the crown. If that's what you and the media want to believe, that's great. Truth is, a Taurus sits on the throne of England, and that's one prized possession.

Taurus babies are cuddly and docile, as long as you don't try to change their schedule, diapers, or diet, until they are ready to be changed. A Taurus toddler who doesn't want to wear his red sweater will either stiffen his entire body so you can't possibly force his little rigid arms into the sleeves or silently let his big eyes fill with tears. Note that the tears never spill. He's trying to manipulate you, even at the tender age of two. He'll bellow if he has to, but instinctively knows that a screaming fit will only get him punished. Exchange the red sweater for his favorite blue one and he will instantly flash an angelic smile and launch his chubby body at you for a hug. Taurus kids don't share. In fact, most prefer to be only children so they have it all.

Taurus siblings never pick up their side of the bedroom, leave wet towels on the bathroom floor, and forget to brush their teeth. On weekends, they sleep until noon, get up, move to the couch, and sleep until bedtime, with an occasional break for whatever they can scrounge from the fridge. You seldom fight, though. You learned at the age of three not to touch their toys, clothes, or the favorite parent of the moment.

What do you do in a family like this? Be polite. Learn to lie. Pretend to listen to your parents' endless lectures, and keep marking off those red X's on your calendar. They may be boring, blathering killjoys, but they've kept you well fed and bought you a decent car for graduation. Keep smiling until you can race off into the sunset.

Office Party—Bitches, Snitches, and the Chronically Inert

The King was in his counting-house,
Counting out his money.

NURSERY RHYME

A Taurus boss seems quiet, predictable, and steady. Never hear your Taurus boss utter a cross word, even when you are late, or call in sick every other Friday? Think she is so wrapped up in her projects that she doesn't notice you spend twenty minutes on the phone, or take an extra half hour at lunch? Your dream world is about to turn into nightmare city.

A Taurus boss notices everything you do and eavesdrops

as much as possible. Think of Ebenezer Scrooge. You will be expected to work as hard as he does, although you are only a salaried slob and he takes home the profits. Taurus bosses will hand out annual merit increases and maybe toss a company Christmas party. But the raise will be minimum and the party in the break room. Don't expect truffles. Do expect a bag of peppermints and a cheap card.

Never sit your coffee cup on this boss's desk or your ass in her chair. Taurus is as possessive at the office as at home. Taurus Oskar Schindler, of *Schindler's List* fame, saved more than a thousand Jews from the Nazis. No one questions his bravery, or his compassion, two definite Taurus traits. However, other signs are as brave and as compassionate. It was Schindler's argument that defined his Taurus character, when he refused to let "his" Jews be taken from his factory.

Bulls are born dictators. The Ayatollah Khomeini and Saddam Hussein are two excellent examples of Taurean bosses on the ludicrous scale. These guys keep score. So does your boss. Time is money. Your time. His money. Sooner or later you'll be presented with a precise list of all the minutes and hours you've stolen and a matching deduction from your final paycheck.

Jangle his or her nerves by rearranging your desk frequently. Wear bright orange or erratic patterns to keep them from standing over your shoulder. Gaslight them by mirroring their uncomprehending stare when they are expounding on the virtues of investing 40 percent of your salary in blue-chip stock. This could, of course, backfire when the boss decides you need a lesson in investment strategies and sends you to an accelerated course in Lubbock, Texas.

Swimming with corporate sharks is dangerous. So is running with bulls. If a determined, stubborn, unchanging Taurus casts her eye on your job, I hope you are a quick-witted Gemini or a meticulous Virgo; otherwise you'll have a marathon race on your hands.

Taurus coworkers are not idea men and women. They are creatures of habit who like to do the same thing day in and day out. They look down on you and everyone else. They don't gossip; they judge. And they spy. Rarely, they will spy for the boss. Usually, they chalk up chits of office chatter for their own benefit. The Taurus employee who climbs the corporate ladder isn't quite as ruthless as a Capricorn attempting a coup, or as patient as a Scorpio willing you to die. They are determined and stubborn and thorough.

The Taurus employee is often underestimated because of her quiet nature. She is not the flash-dash sales rep of the galaxy. Nor is she the flamboyant, desk-thumping debater. She will simply decide she deserves your job and, if you aren't extremely astute and a little paranoid, she will have it. If it's any consolation, she will probably have the boss's office someday, too.

To foil these backstabbers, lock up everything at night. Don't leave a paper on your desk or a file open. Code-key your computer so they can't come in on the weekends and look through your database. Use a headset so you don't have to speak as loudly when on the phone.

To irk them, borrow their staple remover, or favorite pen, without asking. Come in early and be talking on their phone when they arrive. Smile vaguely, ignore their twitching eyelids, and keep talking. Walk around with your own notebook and jot down a couple of words as you pass their desk. Don't trust any of those other morons you work with, either. You never know which one of them might be waiting for the Bull's chair if she gets yours.

Can't We All Get Along?

Wondering how you can survive, let alone thrive? Here are a few tips on how to keep the bullish characters in your life eating out of your hand.

Moody Blue Bulls

Notorious Taurean moods stem from a basic feeling of insecurity. Events as minor as a change in dinner plans, or a disapproving look from you, can send your Bull into a blue funk.

Hugs work nicely for either sex and all ages. So does music, a favorite movie, or a gesture as simple as handing over the remote. Remember the Silence Is Golden rule when your Bull sulks. They usually prefer not to talk when they are upset, so let them alone, set a soft mood of your own, and sooner rather than later they will curl up beside you on the couch and let you scratch them behind the ears.

Stingy Bulls

You can have anything you want, including your name on the checking account (although that may take a little longer), with patience, timing, and a bit of harmless deception. You must learn how to manipulate your Taurus into thinking your wants were his, or her, idea.

Example: You want a new car but bullyboy won't cough up the dough. Rationalizing that your old car is a death trap won't budge him. Wait until he's in his benevolent-dictator mood, the one where he hums that weird little melody and cooks breakfast. Coo over breakfast. Then sigh and give him the worried act. Tell him you don't feel *secure* driving your old car. You understand *he can't afford* a new car, but a nice *used* one would be fine.

Anytime between lunch and the next three days he will assimilate the seeds you plant, replant them in his psyche, and sprout the idea as if it were his own. He'll be worried about you driving that rickety piece of crap. And, only a new car is good enough for his little woman.

Lazy Bulls

Taurus is the laziest sign in the zodiac. Only a Pisces can remain immobile for longer periods of time, for reasons I'll explain later. To keep your Taurus man, woman, or child up and moving takes a bit of strategy. Yelling, belittling, even a beating will only make them dig in their heels and refuse to budge. Remember, human Bulls are uncannily like their zodiac symbol. Tug on a bull's nose ring, and he'll stand firm and blink at you. Coax him with a handful of sweet hay and he'll follow you right into the corral.

Taurus loves a reward. Makes them natural suckers for the stick-and-carrot routine. So, when waving that list of honey-dos, or teen chores at them, make sure to dangle a prize at the end (e.g., "After you do your chores, you can go to the mall with your friends").

A careful explanation of what won't happen also kicks the Bull's butt in gear. However, don't threaten. Be calm and rational—I really want you to have the poker game here tonight, honey. But, there's so much to do beforehand, I'm afraid I'll be too exhausted to go to the movies so you and the boys can have the house to yourself.

Raging Bulls

Unless you are an insane Aquarius, a barroom-brawling Aries, or a surefooted Capricorn who can dodge flying objects, I strongly suggest that you do not further provoke an already bellowing Taurus. Stay quiet, and at arm's length, until they stomp into the bedroom and slam the door. Then head for the kitchen and the microwave brownie mix. Or light a chocolate-scented candle if your Bull is trying out the latest diet fad. Turn on some soothing music and a blue light bulb. Fix yourself a snack, put up your feet, and wait. Unless your Taurus man, woman, or child is seriously wounded, he or she will be unable to resist and will shuffle out, chagrined, to join you.

Quick Tips for Emergencies

- ☿ Bulls need to feel secure.
- ☿ Timing is key to getting your way.
- ☿ When they go ballistic, reach for the chocolate and keep your head down.

♉ Sex will end any fight with this sensual sign.
♉ Gaslight them with your own uncomprehending stare.

Raging Bulls
John Wilkes Booth
Calamity Jane
Gary Condit
Rudolph Hess
Emperor Hirohito of Japan
Ho Chi Minh
Reverend Jim Jones
Timothy McVeigh
Dennis Rodman
Homer Simpson

Chapter Four

Gemini

May 21–June 20

Take Heart, Take Every One

Element: Air. Gemini Air is like a pesky breeze on a day at the beach. It makes you squint, so you don't get a clear picture of what's happening around you.

Quality: Mutable. Gemini is the human version of the revolving door.

Symbol: The Twins. Double-trouble. Double-talk. Double-life. Double-cross.

Ruler: Mercury, the god of mischief and deceit.

Favorite Pastime: Jumping to the wrong conclusion.

Favorite Book: *How to Get Anyone to Agree to Anything.*

Role Model: The Tasmanian Devil.

Dream Job: Gossip columnist.

Key Phrase: "Because I want to."

Body Part: Fingers, usually broken from wagging them in other people's faces.

Approach with Caution

Gemini, the third sign of the zodiac, lives in the House of Communication and Short Trips. Conventional astrology says that Twins are energetic, versatile charmers and intelligent, multitasking, social butterflies. Truth is, being with a Gemini is like being a permanent guest at the Mad Hatter's tea party.

A critical rule is not to confuse Gemini duality with the dual nature of Pisces. Fish swim against one another, which makes Pisces its own worst enemy. Gemini Twins always stand side by side, egging each other on, giving you all kinds of crap. They are crafty versus intellectual, fast-talking con artists versus true philosophers. A Twin's idea of success is to be on the A-list of every big shot in town. They love to stand around at cocktail parties and play the Name Dropping Game. Telling one that you know Paul McCartney's hair stylist will ensure you a place at his or her side during dinner.

Gemini is headstrong, not independent. They skim through life. Twins demand freedom, but it's the freedom of a teenager. They are too busy rebelling to listen to any other point of view. Being born without the objective-assessment gene has voided the ability to see any other opinion but theirs as valid. Argue with one, and suffer an interrogation that could make a trained spy crumble. Win your case, and Gemini will say, "That's just what I was trying to tell you."

If You Love One—Gemini Man

I wouldn't be caught dead marrying a woman old enough to be my wife.

TONY CURTIS (June 3)

He is simply irresistible. The Gemini man is a fun-loving, independent, roguish romantic who has a doctorate in flirting. He can cook an exotic dinner. Then dance with you in the starlight, point out the constellations, and capture your heart with his beautiful version of their myths. Don't invite the wedding guests yet. While you are mentally compiling the guest list, he will excuse himself to get you a fresh glass of chilled wine, and while in the kitchen, manage to phone three other girls for dates next weekend. The only thing this schmoozing, womanizing, party animal is interested in is adding your phone number and bra size to his ever-increasing list of victims.

Gemini movie star Errol Flynn was long regarded as the black sheep of Hollywood. The phrase "in like Flynn" was coined as tribute to his ability to score. His real-life adventures, rebellions, and general unruliness rivaled those of the swashbuckling heroes he portrayed. Flynn was married three times and cheated on all of his wives. His first wife, French actress Lily Damita, said, "You never know when he's telling the truth. He lies for the fun of it."

His life was one of cheerful excess. But, by his late forties, his hurricane-force existence had taken its toll, and he was a burned-out shell of his former, lively self. Flynn died of a heart attack at fifty.

Your Twin will probably not be quite as bad, but all Gemini men have a gypsy moth's fatal attraction to a pretty face. Totally faithful Gems do exist, but are rarer than a shy Sagittarius. In fact, the word *faithful* has a different meaning to a Gemini man. Think of Gemini Brigham Young, the Mormon founder of Salt Lake, who had twenty-seven wives. I'm sure that, in his mind, Brother Brigham considered himself a devoted and faithful husband. In my mind, he was in Gemini Paradise.

Yours will have five hobbies, four careers, and an assortment of friends that resemble a mini–United Nations. But, his intellectual prowess is limited to his memorization of the various versions of Trivial Pursuit and entertaining his friends by tearing you to pieces with his merciless, acerbic tongue. He lives to put down people, and will call you fat ass in public, or snap his fingers at you when his glass is empty.

Cold-hearted and calculating, he is a blatant social climber and will propose on the first date if he smells money. As a husband, he is ambivalent. The only thing this guy's passionate about is being entertained.

If you think love means being together at least some of the time, sharing dinner, and watching the tube, you had better find yourself a homey Cancer, or a quiet Virgo, and send this horny hound dog packing. Or you could look on the bright side. You may be hysterical and freaked out half the time, but you'll never be bored.

If You Love One—Gemini Woman

Well-behaved women rarely make history.

Marilyn Monroe (June 1)

A Gemini woman is a breath of fresh air. She is generous of spirit and heart, and has lots of friends. Her ideal man is original, busy, and has absolutely no desire to pin her down in any way. She is witty, fun loving, and eternally curious. She can systematically juggle a home, a career, family responsibilities, and several hobbies. Before you decide this vivacious whirlwind is for you, understand that her usual hobbies are other men.

A female Twin is the satin-clad, glamorous, sex-using female version of the Hollywood heel. She is her own worst enemy and attracts men who are just as shallow in a classic case of the user being used. She splits her Twin nature, forever chasing a fantasy, while simultaneously looking for Big Daddy.

Consider Gemini Marilyn Monroe. Sex kitten in public, Monroe spent her private life looking for a stable home and a man who would take care of her. However, in true Gemini form, she never allowed anyone to get close enough, or hang around long enough, to establish a lasting relationship. Although she often complained bitterly that no one took her seriously, she was never willing to give up the glamour and attention to seriously pursue any of the intellectual and humanitarian interests her loyal fans claim she supported. In archetypical Gemini-duality, Marilyn lamented that all she wanted was a husband and a home, but she also said, "I have too many fantasies to be a housewife." She oozed sexuality, but if she had any true intellectual bearing, she traded it early on in favor of the spotlight. In an interview at the height of her career she said, "I seem to be a whole superstructure without a foundation."

Of course, your Gemini will be much more stable, and less bimboesque, but she also will be a woman of many interests, all dependent upon her mood of the moment, and what, or whom, she's found to drag home to examine, probe, and/or fall in love with temporarily.

She loves gossip, and her detective skills are superlative. In fact she would make a good private eye, or spy, except for a fatal flaw. While she can keep a secret, she often can't resist sharing juicy bits of gossip, especially if it makes her look good in comparison. If you insist on confessing your own dark past, don't say I didn't warn you.

Gem lives to set things straight. You included. She will smother you with love and devotion—for about five minutes. Then begin the task of changing you for your own good. She will toss at you with hurricane force books, tapes, seminars, advice, and examples from her own life. She will find you a job, a counselor, and an in-patient facility and expect a progress report each evening.

Auntie Mame, the story of a freewheeling, live-life-to-the-hilt, independent woman, is the ultimate portrait of the Gemini female. Superstar Rosalind Russell won a Golden Globe and was nominated for an Academy Award for her portrayal of this madcap lady. Perhaps that was because Russell was a Gemini and recognized the character on a soul level. The movie's tag line, "Life is a banquet and most poor suckers are starving to death!" sums up Ms. Gemini's philosophy in a nutshell.

If You Are One-Born Rotten

Can we talk?

Joan Rivers (June 8)

You belong to the Fad-of-the-Month club. You were the first kid on your block to have a hula hoop, a skateboard, or roller blades. You are also the first one to arrive in the Emergency Room with a broken bone, because you refused to wear protective gear. You have a hundred acquaintances but few friends. Probably because you spend half of your time talking behind their backs and the other half making eyes at their lovers.

Gems make good writers, mimics, used-car salesmen, con artists, and magpies. You are also one of the psychic signs, but can't shut up long enough to practice your meditation exercises.

You love to embellish the boring details of your life. What starts out as a trip to the grocery store becomes the day you spotted Elvis in the parking lot. When you confronted him, you discovered it wasn't the King after all—it was Jimmy Hoffa.

You do have a gift for imparting knowledge to others. On the playground you were the one who taught the other kids how to play doctor. If you were a drug, it would be speed.

You hate solitude. You aren't introspective and need the stimulus of other people to help manage the buzzing noises in your head. It has been said of Gemini Bob Hope that if he could live his life over again, he wouldn't have the time. While this description neatly fits every Gemini, the reason your social calendar is overbooked is because, when there's no one else to talk to, you bore yourself to sleep.

In Gemini, Mercury bestows a natural talent for pot stirring. You love to invite over for drinks people who detest each other, then sit back and watch the mayhem.

Your Achilles Heel is romance. You are a sucker for a sob story, flattery, or an out-and-out lie. In any other area of life, you are suspicious of most people who offer genuine friendship because you are such a phony baloney. However, if someone listens intently to your latest goofy scheme, interjects a bit of his, or her, own pathos now and then, you are hooked. Never mind that your latest flame is your sixth spouse. You instantly fall in love, then after the smoke clears and you realize you've chosen yet another card-carrying psycho, you run like Hell. If you could learn to not get married in between the loving and the running, you'd save yourself many headaches.

Your breezy nature and impressive recuperative powers keep you relatively unscathed in matters of the heart. If you have guilt at all, it's more a nagging sense that you should have more emotional empathy. But it really doesn't matter. You are protected by Mercury, the god of thieves and liars, and seldom get hoisted on your own petard.

There isn't a nose in the zodiac you can't tweak. You laugh in the face of Raging Bull and were born with the ability to give Virgo ulcers. You make Aries see double red and outtalk Sagittarius. You pop Leo's arrogance balloon with a well-timed bit of truth. And, stodgy Capricorn's pointed barbs shatter against your cool demeanor. The Water signs' blatant emotionalism drives you bonkers. However, you know just how to skewer Fish, Crabs, and Scorpions and serve them à la carte. You and the other Air signs, Aquarius and Libra, understand each other on a soul level, and therefore, rarely have serious confrontations.

Your philosophy is, "Do something, even if it's wrong." You may run into a brick wall and get the wind knocked out of you. But your energy scatters around the obstacle to gather again, whole, on the other side. Let the rest of humanity lumber along like elephants on parade. You dart through life adding color and imagination. Years from now when all your old lovers are shuffling along behind their walkers, you'll be writing your three-volume set of memoirs and teaching tap dancing on the side just to keep your body limber.

It's ALL Relative—The Gemini Family

There was about seven of us in a two-bedroom apartment. And you know, we all used to walk around in our boxers, half naked.

Munky (James Shaffer, June 6)

Living in a Gemini-ruled household is like living in the city room of the *Daily Planet*. The air crackles with humor, drama, and heated discussions. Ringing phones, slamming doors, TVs, radios, and video games add to the noise.

Your Gemini home will be eternally cluttered with Mom's latest kitchen-table business and Dad's old high school buddies. Books, magazines, and newspapers will line the walls, be piled in the corners, and cover every available inch of table space. The good news is that by the time you start kindergarten, you will be reading at high school level; the bad news is, if you are allergic to dust, you'll need a breathing machine.

Most likely, you will either be an only child or have only one brother or sister. Gemini seldom have lots of kids because they don't make the best parents on the planet. That's because your Gemini parents have such endlessly long childhoods themselves. Your friends will love your folks because they let them smoke and drink at your house. Whether or not you think this is a good idea is irrelevant and immaterial to your Twin parents since they believe in freedoms of every kind.

Your Gemini mom may not be the best housekeeper under the sun, but that's because she's too busy taking yoga, teaching you piano, and reading the latest mystery novel all after a hard day's work at the office. Dad will try to be a good father, but he would rather be your pal and teach you how to pick a winner at the racetrack than about the birds and bees.

Gemini babies are twice as alert, smart, and mischievous as other babies. Your Gemini toddler has more disappearing acts than a magician and will keep you in peak physical shape running after him or her. Buy yours a kiddie harness unless you like running through the mall trying to find your little Twin who's decided to investigate all the interesting shops and people on his own.

Your Gemini teen will insist that he, or she, can study to the sound of the latest rock group, and it's true. Encourage them to learn everything thoroughly, as their quick minds absorb ideas instantly, but have little use for detail. Teach your Twin early about the value of making a schedule and sticking to it. They will balk, interrupt, fidget, and look like they are sitting on the electric chair. But they will also remember and use your advice when they have bitten off more than they can chew and don't want to look lame in front of their friends.

Gemini brothers have new girlfriends every week and seem to have phones growing out of their heads. Sister Gem will use every trick to get you to let her borrow your purple sweater with the silver beads. She seems to cry and smile simultaneously. If you don't let her borrow it, she will sneak in your room later and take it anyway. Twin siblings fill the house with friends, parties, and lots of noise. Both have a ruthless sense of humor that you'll suffer sooner or later. Both have the gift of exaggeration, and neither will let you escape their wild tales.

Surviving a Gemini family depends entirely upon you. Since your parents are eternal teens themselves, they will give you as much freedom as you can handle to learn everything you want to learn. If you're smart, by the time you are ready for college, you'll be able to skip ahead two years.

Office Party—Bitches, Snitches, and the Chronically Inert

> *Everything in life to me is a psychological game, a series of challenges you either meet or don't. I am always testing people who work for me.*
>
> DONALD TRUMP (JUNE 14)

Working for a Gemini boss is either a breeze or a tempest. One morning she will arrive twenty minutes early, go through everyone's desk, and spend the rest of the day pacing around looking over your shoulder. The next she won't notice whether you are diligently typing or talking to your boyfriend on the phone. The catch, and there always is one with Gemini, is that you will never be able to guess which Twin will show up. That's because she doesn't know, either.

Your boss will have a speakerphone so he can pace while talking or rummage through the disorganized mess on his desk for the contract he's discussing. He's very accessible and will have a pager, cell phone, car phone, and a phone in his shower at home in case you need him to solve a midnight crisis. The down side is that he expects you to be just as accessible.

He's reckless. Yours may not lose two fortunes within the space of a few short years, like Gemini Donald Trump, but he will takes chances, especially when other executives push for caution.

A Gemini boss likes mind games and can severely test your resolve with a series of questions designed to ferret out company secrets and judge your ability to think on your feet. Telling a Gemini employer, "Because that's the way we've always done it," is grounds for summary dismissal. The rules and players in a Gemini-run office change faster than you can print new nametags.

With a little timing and a bit of courage, you can have some fun getting even. Let those monotonous, detailed little tasks and projects pile up for a couple of weeks. Pick a time when Boss Twin has been exceptionally banal and demanding, then ask for a "few minutes" of time. Review every item as methodically as an Earth sign reviewing the annual budget, making sure you take up most of the afternoon. Your boss will probably dash out the door as soon as you stand up and may even take off the next day or two. Of course this could backfire, as a Gemini is quick to spot a plot because he, or she, is at the bottom of so many. In that case, you could find yourself rearranging those damnable filing cabinets on Saturday.

Having a Gemini coworker is like working with the invisible man. Twins are rarely at their desks because they are too busy schmoozing in the next department, ferreting out the latest gossip over the water cooler, or chatting over coffee in the boss's office. Geminis are not into clock watching, so they are frequently late to work. They also refuse to work overtime, because their personal life is always more important. Since their paychecks are always short, Gems are constantly putting the touch on everyone for a few bucks to tide them over until payday.

A Gemini in search of a new desk is a master of duplicity. He, or she, will use the new-best-friend approach to avoid open conflict. They will cozy up, learn everything you do, steal your ideas, then hand you a carefully crafted efficiency report that's just ambiguous enough to make you look inefficient. They will lie that the boss told them to prepare it, then magnanimously offer to switch positions in order to "save" your employment. This is done in such a silver-tongued way that you may be tempted to fall for the Twin charm. Don't. As soon as they flit out the door thinking they've nailed you, go straight to your boss and expose the sneaky plan.

To irk one, act as if you know something they don't. Gems can't stand secrets of any kind and will tramp all over the office quizzing your coworkers, while you retype that position description.

Can't We All Get Along?

Think you need track shoes to keep up with a Gemini? Not so, once you know what makes them run.

Overextended Twins

Gemini men, women, and children have the highest natural energy levels in the Universe. Their Air element, doubled by their Twin nature, makes them the most restless, sensation-sensitive of all the signs. They can drive themselves to exhaustion and then be unable to unwind.

To keep yours from having a nervous breakdown, help create a space where he or she can retreat and relax. It can be a corner of the living room where your Gem can sit and read but still feel included in the family activities, a work space in the garage, or a home office in the spare bedroom.

Long, private soaks in the bath for your adult Twin help quiet a buzzing brain. Lavender-scented sheets, gentle back rubs, and a simple home-cooked meal work for everyone.

Fickle Twins

Keeping a Gemini faithful is not such an intimidating feat, once you understand that while they may demand freedom, they crave a safe, stable home and a partner who listens. Gems love to share their adventures and to hear about yours as well. Lingering over dinner while your Twin entertains you with the latest buzz at work, or juicy gossip, will ensure that the communication lines stay open.

Gems love surprises. Short getaways and unexpected notes or gifts prove that you are thinking of them. Create a safe haven, let them roam the neighborhood, stay out late with their friends, and just like a housecat, a Gemini will always return to snuggle down beside you.

Cagey Twins

It's been said that all Gemini have kissed the Blarney stone, and they all were certainly born with a con artist's heart. However, even the most outrageous Gemini is basically honest (due to a horror of being confined in small spaces, such as jail cells), so you can easily steer yours away from his or her more dangerous ideas with a simple reminder of the consequences.

But no Gemini alive can resist the urge to exaggerate a story. Gems love to plot, plan, and pretend and have a wicked sense of humor. Laughing at their plans to get the boss fired or their scheme to sabotage the ATM so it spits money like a slot machine safely satisfies their urge to stretch the truth, and provides you with hours of great entertainment.

Slapdash Twins

Gemini is the most versatile sign in the zodiac. However, anxiety is the force that drives them. Gemini fear that if they don't keep moving, everything they are juggling will come crashing down.

Twins skim a topic instead of learning it thoroughly and often proceed on nerve alone when they should study harder. If they misjudge the person they want to impress, or the depth of their history test, and expose themselves as a fraud, you will have a most miserable creature on your hands. Few things are worse to a Twin than appearing ignorant.

Give adults an electronic calendar, which will satisfy their penchant for gadgets, and keep them organized so they can give themselves time to do an in-depth report instead of bullet-point outline for that marketing presentation. Set aside uninterrupted study time for young Twins, while you still have some control over their actions, to help develop good research skills they can use for a lifetime.

Quick Tips for Emergencies

Ⅱ Twins need to communicate.
Ⅱ Listening is key to understanding them.

II Quell a mood with a night on the town.

II Praise their ideas.

II Gaslight them by acting as if you know something they don't.

Good Twin, Bad Twin

Boy George

Joan Collins

Jeffrey Dahmer

Ian Fleming (creator of James Bond)

Anne Heche

John Hinckley, Jr.

Dr. Jack Kevorkian

Marquis de Sade

Prince

Dr. Ruth Westheimer

Chapter Five

Cancer

June 21–July 22

Step Into My Parlor

Element: Water. Cancer Water slogs through shifting quicksand. You think you are strolling the sunniest of beaches. Soon, you are clawing your way out of a life-sucking black hole.

Quality: Cardinal. Cancer's leadership qualities are confined to head emotional manipulator.

Symbol: The Crab. Crabby. Furtive. Reclusive. Brittle.

Ruler: The Moon. Shadowy character. Behind-the-scene maneuvers. Loony bird. Lunatic.

Favorite Pastime: Whining.

Favorite Book: *The Martyr's Handbook.*

Role Model: Eeyore.

Dream Job: Professional victim.

Key Phrase: "After all I've done for you."

Body Part: Breasts, permanently chaffed from the hair shirt.

Cancer, the fourth sign of the zodiac, lives in House of Home. Feel-good astrology promotes Cancer as private, nurturing, and deeply committed to family and friends. Truth is Crabs are oblique, manipulating, and should *be* committed by their families and friends.

All Water signs are sensitive, but Cancer wallows in emotional turmoil. The Moon rules Cancer, and pulls on the emotional structure of the Crab in the same manner as it causes the tides to rise and fall, but speeds up the process. Their moods change hourly. Crabs can laugh, sob, sulk, joke, retreat, attack, and complain all within a twenty-four-hour period. Remember that when you feel the need to rescue one. You could go to bed with Betty Crocker and wake up with Lizzie Borden.

Most are pathologically shy in public. Occasionally, you'll find one in the closet at home, hugging a box of emergency junk food rations, reading an earthquake preparedness manual. They are jumpy. Sudden movements panic them and most are afraid of crickets, frogs, grasshoppers, and the Easter Bunny. They have been known to run themselves to exhaustion trying to flee their own shadows.

Cancers are touchy, not logical. By taking offense at the first sign of disagreement, they walk through life with an everyone's-out-to-get-me attitude. Being born without the rational-thinking gene clouds their ability to look at themselves objectively. Argue with one, and she will scuttle under the nearest rock to avoid conflict. But, be warned: they are not defeated, just plotting their next maneuver. Let down your guard, and you may lose a toe.

If You Love One-Cancer Man

*I hate to advocate drugs, alcohol, violence or insanity to anyone,
but they've always worked for me.*

HUNTER S. THOMPSON (JULY 18)

The first thing you'll notice is his genuine, and adorable, smile. The Cancer man is sweet, chivalrous, and has a wonderfully offbeat sense of humor that can be downright loony. He is sentimental, sensual, and truly affectionate. He is a traditionalist who respects the proprieties of courtship, believes in family and forever, and he's absolutely the best snuggle-bunny in the Universe.

You may see an ideal mate, but what you get is an ideal stalker. A male Crab's idea of devotion is bonding at the hip, so unless you are prepared to become his Siamese twin, run in the opposite direction as fast as possible. In bed he is tender, but so passive that you'll soon tire of always being on top.

His devotion is legendary. However, don't say "I do" until you understand that this extends to every friend and relative he's ever had, especially Mother. It's not above him to wait until the honeymoon to tell you she's coming to live with you as soon as you return.

He's subjective. His favorite game is Guess How I'm Feeling? You will be expected to read his mind, sense his moods, and mend his fragile ego, all without benefit of knowing what has upset him. Don't worry. Everything upsets him. Forget to buy toothpaste, and he'll decide you don't love him anymore. Say you want a night out with the girls, and he'll expect divorce papers in the morning.

Conversely, he will be so blind to your feelings that you will soon find yourself thinking of ways to escape. Try talking rationally and he will become morose and overemotional. He's so preoccupied with his own sensibilities, and his basic character is so convoluted, that he simply can't believe you don't feel exactly as he does on every issue. He's as moody as the female Crab, and punishes any perceived slight by retreating into his metaphorical shell to pout.

Consider Cancer Ross Perot's run for the presidency. Perot prided himself on playing daddy, boss, and teacher to us less enlightened folks. When faced with the inevitable opposition, he took it as a personal affront; packed up his charts, graphs, and pointer; and went home. In typical Cancer fashion, after a suitable period of withdrawal (e.g., punishing those who would not see his light), he decided he might jump back in the political ring if asked. I suppose he's still waiting.

The male Crab is as paranoid about security as the Bull but, in a financial crisis, will expect you to do all that nasty stuff like making a budget or working two jobs to ensure the family's future. He'll be too ill with a case of stressed-induced acne to show his face in public.

He will stop at nothing to get you to agree with his point of view, even if it's only on the best flavor of ice cream. Anything less is total rejection. First, he will explain in excruciating detail why pecan is better than black walnut. Next he'll try his rote lost-boy look to win your acquiescence. If neither tactic works, he will sigh, say he's not hungry, and sit brooding in front of the TV. You better be prepared to either give in or live in silence. Before you gratefully choose the latter, remember silence to a Crab is punctuated with long, mournful sighs, minor to major groans, and frequent whimpering mutters.

A prime example of a male Crab in action is King Henry VIII. When Henry wanted to divorce his first wife, Catherine (a Sagittarius), in order to marry Gemini Anne Boleyn, you would think that he would have said, "So be it." Instead, in typical Cancer style, Henry tried to ensure that everyone in the kingdom agreed with him. He dragged out the barge, visiting his royal advisors up and down the Thames. He petitioned the Pope for an annulment, even encouraged Catherine to say their marriage was never consummated.

When Catherine refused, he locked her in the Tower of

London. When the Pope refused, King Crab created the Church of England, installing himself as its secular head. Through alternating displays of temperament and torture, he secured most of his noblemen's support. Then, true to his changeable nature, he had Anne beheaded, in just under three years of marriage, after it had taken him five years to fight the battle to marry her in the first place.

While your Crab will probably not have you dispatched, he is totally capable of blinding himself to everything that doesn't reflect his narrow, ever-changing viewpoint. And you will suffer a tedious display of relentless carping and whining aimed at securing your slavish, unquestioning devotion.

Since you're in a no-win situation anyway, you might as well tell him you like boysenberry sherbet, you've just quit your job, and by the way, is that a pimple sprouting on the end of his nose?

If You Love One—Cancer Woman

I understand my people better than anyone. I study them all the time and even conduct experiments.

IMELDA MARCOS (JULY 2)

Kind and mothering, the Cancer woman instantly makes you think of apple pie and a crackling fire. Your lady Crab has a delightful, whimsical sense of humor and a generous, compassionate heart. She expects a man who is faithful, thoughtful, and stable. Her life revolves around you, family, and a select circle of friends.

Before you try to sweep her off her dainty little feet, you might reread the old poem *The Spider and the Fly*. A female Crab weaves what appears to be a cozy love nest, complete with devoted companion. Set one hairy little foot inside, and you'll get stuck in a tangle of emotional blackmail forever.

Your home will be a shrine to her life-to-date. The walls are covered with pictures of relatives, friends, and the clown she met when she was three. Every Cancer woman has a box stashed somewhere that's full of single earrings, corks from wine bottles, seashells, postcards, and at least one of her baby teeth.

She is emergency-phobic. Her car will be packed with a first aid kit, dried fruit and trail mix, bottled water, pillows, and a homing beacon in case you are ever lost in the desert. The fact that you live at the beach and she rides a bicycle to work is of no consequence.

She's so vague that it's often hard to tell if she is listening intently or sleeping with her eyes open. And, although she will cry profusely and apologize because she spilled coffee on your autographed poster of Mark McGwire when she took it off the wall to dust behind it, you will never know whether it was an accident or your punishment for staying out too late with your friends last week.

Being true to her Crabby character, Lizzie Borden at first ignored her new stepmother. When that didn't work, she resorted to a series of calculated and well-timed emotional out-bursts. Ever the maneuvering Crab, Lizzie waged a behind-the-scenes war of wills while her public image remained one of pious Sunday school teacher and benefactress. I doubt that she planned the double murder. I theorize that her frustrated inability to drive an emotional wedge between hated step-mother and beloved father finally exploded into a megacase of Cancer hysterics. Remember that if you are determined to wed one of these moody, clinging, moon-ruled lunatics.

Lady Crab is a grazer. To win her, keep your pantry stocked with fattening, filling food of no nutritional value. Her idea of a good home-cooked meal is potatoes and gravy, biscuits and jelly, and a double hot fudge Twinkie-split.

Your Crab may fool you into thinking she wants you to take charge, but in reality she will control you through a series of well-executed near-death experiences, various psychosomatic illnesses, and regular 2 A.M. visits to the emergency room. Any remaining time will be spent reminding you of her many sacrifices on your ungrateful behalf over the years.

Her anger is part tragic queen and part shrewd manipulator. Call to say you have a late meeting, and your Crab will whisper, "That's OK. I understand." Before you hang up she will tell you how long she slaved over your favorite meal despite a blinding headache. Oh, and there's no aspirin in the house. She hoped you could stop and pick some up on the way home, but she supposes she will live until you get home. Imagine weak laughter at this point. You will feel like a jerk for the rest of the evening. She, on the other hand, will hang up the phone, smile, fix herself a plate of leftovers and flip on the TV. On the surface, a female Crab always seems so harmless. So did Lizzie.

If You Are One-Born Rotten

All our final resolutions are made in a state of mind which is not going to last.

MARCEL PROUST (JULY 10)

Home is your hiding place, where you can remain locked inside for several months having your groceries delivered. If you do stick out your head, a sudden breeze can send you scurrying back to your darkened room. However, you don't care because you plan on making it rich from a home-based business driven by computer links and the telephone.

You need no social interaction and have few friends. The ones you do have you treat as helpless children to be mothered and smothered. You are not into sports, since walking to the refrigerator for one of your five-dozen daily snacks tires you. Your dietary habits could kill a Taurus, yet you manage to live to a ripe old age.

You have such a morbid fear that Big Brother is watching that your shades are always drawn so "they" can't look in. You realize you are paranoid, but rationalize that that doesn't mean someone isn't really out to get you. You, on the other hand, constantly spy on everyone you know. You should really try to get a grip on reality while you can still find the handle.

Crabs make good double agents, stalkers, antiques dealers, real estate brokers, and shut-ins. You are also natural-born actors and make great caretakers of the sick and demented.

You pride yourself on making things last and are still apt to be driving your first car, exterior carefully preserved with carnauba wax and interior still like new under several layers of blankets. You cling to old romantic partners with the same tenacity.

You are a hypochondriac and so susceptible to suggestion that I strongly advise you to never watch the Operation Channel. If Uncle Joe in Flatfoot, Georgia, has gallstones, you crawl around on the floor for a week in agony. Your home library is full of medical textbooks, holistic medicine journals, and various guides to a healthier lifestyle. You keep a copy of *Gray's Anatomy* on your nightstand, right next to the tray of antacids, tranquilizers, sleeping pills, and liniments. You know the hotline number of every quack doctor, medicine man, and psychic healer within a hundred miles.

You are usually clean, but chronically rumpled as you keep all your clothes in a pile on the closet floor because you are too cheap to use a professional laundry and too afraid to use the iron.

Your moods change so fast that, even if you managed to work up enough energy to invite your sweetheart over for dinner, by the time you've finished lighting the candles and opening the wine, you've lost interest.

Like Scorpio and Taurus, you too are a collector. The difference is that Taurus collects possessions, Scorpio collects people, and you collect tokens of memories. Like the wad of gum you stepped in on your first date.

You are also tenacious, determined, and stubbornly cling to

what you know in your heart is right, no matter how fero-
ciously others try to dissuade you. Practice meditating to calm
your inner fears and control your urge to hover over every
action of your family and friends, and you'll succeed on every
level.

Your ability to confuse and irritate every other sign assures
your place at the head of the maneuver table. Neither growl-
ing Leo nor fire-breathing Aries can penetrate your tough,
protective shell, and your owlish stare and polished sidestep
drives Sagittarius to self-immolation. You snap off Gemini,
Libra, and Aquarius' Air supply with a few well-chosen observations about their insolent and rude behavior. One of your
frosty stares quickly silences Earth signs Capricorn and Taurus' bleating and bellowing. And Virgo's nitpicky criticism is
no match for your cool assessment of their self-serving faults.
You and the other Water signs, Pisces and Scorpio, understand
each other on a soul level and, therefore, rarely have serious
confrontations.

Yours is the philosophy of "Patience is a virtue." You are
prepared to wait and plan for the future you want. And you
are neither weak nor helpless when confronted by adversity.
Let everyone else posture, preen, and vie for the spotlight.
You are too busy diligently and quietly working behind the
scenes planting the seeds for a bountiful future. Years from
now when your foes are wheeling themselves to therapy in the
geriatric ward, you'll be snug as a bug in your cottage by the
sea, feasting on chocolate tacos and port wine.

It's ALL Relative—The Cancer Family

Never go to bed mad. Stay up and fight.

PHYLLIS DILLER (JULY 17)

Living in a Cancer-ruled family is like living with the ensem-
ble cast of a Greek tragedy. Someone always has hurt feelings,

is in a mood, has a headache, or is waiting for the other shoe to drop.

Get a "C" on a test and your Cancer mom will put one hand on her breast, sink down on the nearest chair, and ask herself what she did wrong in raising you. Try to cut the apron strings for a life of your own, and she'll fake a heart condition to keep you home.

Dad is either aloof and crabby or the life of the party. Either way, he won't get around to telling you the facts of life or showing you how to balance a checkbook. This isn't because he doesn't care; it's because he can't bear to think that someday you will leave home. He will be a loving and patient father who will do everything but let you grow up. Dad Crab would be perfectly content to remodel the basement, the attic, or turn the garage into an apartment if he thought it would keep you there.

Cancer parents will wait up, hovering near the phone, and call 911 and every hospital in town if you are fifteen minutes late from a date. They are the original worrywarts. They also will save your first tooth and squash-stained bib, stuff you with homemade pasta, and affectionately coo over your baby pictures until you are fifty. And, until they are dead, they will meddle in every facet of your life.

Take care when bringing home a sweetheart for parental approval. If they like the person, and you break up, they are capable of keeping your old flame's picture on the piano and will wistfully sigh in its direction if you dare to introduce someone new.

Cancer babies are born with their mood gene turned on high. Cranky little Crabs will expect to be rocked to sleep until they start school and to hold your hand until they are adults.

Cancer siblings cry at the drop of a hat, and you will hurt their feelings no matter what you do. They will also fall down just before Dad walks in the door and start howling that you pushed them. They expect to tag along despite the fact that you are the youngest and will pout should you go out without them. They will constantly try to boss you around, offering their opinions, advice, warnings, and ideas. They will also keep in touch long after you've both left home and will always have a hot meal and a warm bed ready, should you ever need them.

Your Cancer home may be emotional, and boringly old-fashioned, but it's also safe, snug, and filled with family tradition. When you finally do leave, your weeping parents are likely to hand you a little blue checkbook with a surprisingly large figure neatly printed in the balance column.

Office Party—Bitches, Snitches, and the Chronically Inert

> *Things are more like they are now than they have ever been.*
>
> GERALD FORD (JULY 14)

Cancer is not the best sign to have in a power position of any kind. Crab bosses understand their weaknesses, and if yours is in over her or his head, God help everyone in the office. They don't hold up well when the heat is on, and usually do one of two things. Overreact and start a war or retreat behind a closed office door, leaving you and your colleagues to sink or swim on your own.

A Cancer boss will subject you to endless rule changes, withering looks, and testy remarks. Ask for help, and you will be told "figure it out yourself" as an answer. Or you'll get a specific, detailed answer, which will prove to be wrong, then you'll be blamed for the mistake because your Cancer boss will have conveniently forgotten that he gave the order. Since he can't take responsibility for his own actions, he may even write you up, or fire you, to save his ass.

If a formerly unfriendly Crab suddenly wants to be your best friend, you can bet your floppy disks that he, or she, is out to get you, because this type of behavior suggests that they feel guilty about something—like snooping through your trash the night before and telling the boss she found your descriptive, four-letter e-mail. Once you are on alert, it's easy to foil her plans.

Cancer is the most easily confused sign in the zodiac. When the marketing report arrives, date it, log it, and keep a copy for your file. Send only the first page to the backstabber, tell the boss it's on her desk, then sit back and watch the fun as she tries to find the rest.

Gaslight her by using her hypochondria. Greet her first thing in the morning with a tale of the latest nasty flu bug epidemic. At noon say, "Are you feeling well? You look pale." Soon she will begin to sigh, flutter, and crumble. She'll leave early wheezing and coughing, and if you are lucky, will call in sick for the rest of the week.

Can't We All Get Along?

Short of taking a crash course in abnormal psychology or having a key to the neighborhood pharmacy, is it possible to find happiness with the moodiest person in the Universe? Not only is it easy; with a little help from a friend, it's a snap.

Snapping Crabs

Cancers are *the* moodiest sign. They are also the most sensitive and internalize every issue. Help yours cope by offering simple kindness and frequent cuddles. They like to hold hands in front of the fire and watch old movies that make them cry. If they are really in a funk, put them in a warm bath and wash their backs while they sip a cup of herbal tea, then jump into bed. Soon you both will be smiling.

Manipulating Martyr Crabs

Crabs are slow to trust and very suspicious. Their maneuvering and martyrdom is a self-defense mechanism to test your worthiness. Yes, it's exasperating, but easy to overcome. Reassurance is the key. It won't take long to figure out what sets off yours, anything from forgetting the celery to being introduced to one of your good-looking coworkers. No matter how weird your Crab gets, keep declaring your undying love, and soon he or she will relax that death grip and let you out to play with your friends.

Paranoid Crabs

Crabs fear the unknown. They also have wild imaginations and dream up all sorts of scary scenarios that end with them alone and suffering. If you are late, they imagine a crash on the highway. Take a plane trip, and they chew their nails until you call to announce your safe arrival. Purchasing cell phones for the whole family will provide the anchor your Crab needs and is well worth the cost in saving your sanity. And they won't call very much, because the knowledge that they can if they want to quells their fear.

Hypochondriac Crabs

Cancers' emotional fragility, coupled with the fact that they mother everyone in the Universe but themselves, makes them susceptible to real illness. Add their own ultramoody nature, and you have a person who is not only likely to become legitimately sick but one who is extremely capable of making him-, or herself sick.

If your Crab starts to wilt, bundle him or her up in a cozy sweater and head for a movie, an expensive home tour, or the nearest Japanese garden. Provide a pink antacid tablet, drive snuggled together like when you were teenagers, and keep up a running conversation of all his or her favorite memories. Soon your Crab will cast off the sweater and the sick face and happily chat with you about the endless minutiae she loves.

Quick Tips for Emergencies

- ☺ Crabs need reassurance.
- ☺ Cuddle them when they are blue.
- ☺ Encourage their off-beat brand of humor.
- ☺ Remember they are nicest just before attacking.
- ☺ Gaslight them by feeding their hypochondria.

Attack Crabs

John Dillinger
Leona Helmsley
Courtney Love
Nancy Reagan
Tokyo Rose
O. J. Simpson
Clarence Thomas
Mike Tyson
The Werewolf

Chapter Six

Leo

July 23–August 22

My Way, or the Highway

Element: Fire. Leo Fire is the steady, white-hot flame of the Sun. From a distance, it warms. Up close, you fry.

Quality: Fixed. Leo is fixed in its high opinion of itself.

Symbol: The Lion. Lionize. Lion's share. King of the Jungle.

Ruler: The Sun. Sunbathe. Sunstroke. Sunburn.

Favorite Pastime: Giving orders.

Favorite Book: *Intimidation Made Easy.*

Role Model: Foghorn Leghorn.

Dream Job: Boss of bosses.

Key Phrase: "You had it coming."

Body Part: Wrist, permanently sprained from shooting craps for lunch money.

Approach with Caution

Leo the Lion is the fifth sign of the zodiac and lives in the House of Creativity and Sex. Any astrology book will tell you that Leos are proud, self-assured, exuberant fun lovers who are loyal, generous, and elegant. A Leo astrologer wrote those books. Truth is, Lions are attention-grabbing, overbearing egomaniacs whose childish, self-centered behavior is exceeded only by their obnoxious attempts to boss around everyone else.

The Sun rules Leo, and just as it is the center of our Universe, the Lion considers him- or herself the center of yours. They expect outright worship, but will settle for reverent deference to their place as Supreme Ruler. Leos are either loud, brash, and pushy or quiet, dignified, and crafty. Don't mistake quiet for shy. There are no shy Lions.

Leos are theatrical, not practical. Their constant need for attention often negates their playful, happy natures. And when they lose contact with that part of themselves, they become selfish tyrants roaring through life creating misery. Being born with the instant-gratification gene overshadows any ability to understand the value of nurturing an idea or a relationship. Argue with one, and they'll roar with indignant fury. Win your argument, and the Lion will silently stare at you, then retreat into the shadows to plan its next attack.

If You Love One-Leo Man

I make it up all different every time I'm asked.

ANDY WARHOL (August 6)

A Leo male is warm hearted, generous, and dignified. He's a genuine romantic you won't have to tempt twice to go for a moonlit stroll or to your favorite hideaway for the weekend.

The Lion seeks a mate who is stable, family oriented, and intelligent. His family adores him, he keeps his friends laughing, and he's always the center of attention. In the office. In jail. At the beach. He's the center of attention. Always.

His favorite game is Commander-in-Chief. A Leo will snap off orders with the crispness of a general ordering his troops and expect you to move at double time to wait on him hand and foot. He demands to be rewarded for coming home in the evening and he demands your respect, whether he deserves it or not. Should he remember your birthday, nothing but a blatant display of fawning will satisfy his ego.

He rarely loses his temper as long as you call him "master" while bowing in respect. Challenge his authority, and he will roar, kick the sofa, and issue a couple of ultimatums designed to strike fear in your heart. As soon as the scene is over, everything is forgotten. Be stupid enough to deliberately wound a Lion's pride or, worse, attack his dignity, and you'll soon feel like a pound of ground round being sized up for dinner.

If he's a quiet Lion, he'll be a benevolent dictator who wants you to hover over him constantly. He'll want you to rub his aching shoulders and tell him how fit, strong, and wonderful he is, no matter what his age or physical condition. He, on the other hand, will not hesitate to tell you that your hair is a mess, your ass is too big, and that you have the intelligence of a gnat. When you burst into tears, he will be genuinely shocked because, in his mind, he was only trying to give you the benefit of his wise counsel.

Study the character of Professor Henry Higgins in Leo George Bernard Shaw's play *Pygmalion* if you want an object lesson in the character of a male Lion. After berating, humiliating, and lecturing Eliza Doolittle, he refuses to praise her efforts and, instead, takes credit for her success. In typical Leonine befuddlement, Higgins runs shouting for his mother when the girl finally tells him to get lost. Eliza had to be a Capricorn.

In a playful mood, the Lion may act like a clown, but there's nothing easygoing about his nature. Tell him he's being silly, and his mood will change faster than a Cancer under the full moon. Leo wants an audience, not a critic.

He's cocky. At his worst, he's a combination of Felix the Cat and Napoleon on steroids. He'll wear dark glasses at night and make passes at anything that walks, crawls, or slithers. He'll spend money faster than you can earn it. And by the time he's forty, will resemble an aging teenage hoodlum with his beer gut hanging over his too-tight Levi's.

It's said that Leo men always look taller than they really are. This is because they all wear either shoes with lifts or cowboy boots with four-inch heels. Leo shorty Napoleon Bonaparte invented high-heeled shoes for himself, not Josephine.

He will drive a monster pickup that you have to use a ladder to climb into. When he skids into your driveway after knocking over the mailbox, he'll lean on the horn until you appear, then kick the passenger door open with one of his four-hundred-dollar steel-toed boots. Ever the gallant, when he notices he can't see your eyes over the running board, he'll jump out to assist you, and gleefully chant, "Gropin' and Hopin'," while standing behind you.

His vanity knows no bounds. He'll have a tattoo on his butt and not hesitate to drop his drawers at the poolroom to show it off. He, of course, thinks he's the world's greatest lover, which he announces to anyone within a ten-decibel range. However, there's really very little to be said. Two words do come to mind—*frequent* and *enthusiastic.* His definition of foreplay is "Get in the truck."

Everything about a male Lion is exaggerated. Leo Diamond Jim Brady not only had a huge appetite for food but for lavish excess as well. True to his Leonine nature, Diamond Jim was the most flamboyant character of his time. The owner of his favorite restaurant called Brady his "best twenty-five customers." Brady regularly tipped one hundred dollar bills for two-dollar taxi rides, and his famous collection of thirty complete sets of jewelry was estimated at the time in excess of one million dollars. Diamond Jim was just as extravagant in love. He had a dozen gold-plated bicycles made so he and long-time girlfriend Lillian Russell could cruise Central Park in style. Her favorite bike had handlebars covered with mother-of-pearl and spokes decorated with rubies and sapphires. In true Leo style, Diamond Jim was both vulgar and magnificent.

Whether yours is a stuffy, overbearing egotist or a wild and woolly jungle cat, the key to taming a Lion is knowing how to react. Next time he's snarling, lecturing, and posturing in the kitchen because dinner is five minutes late, ignore the fit, smile, and tell him how nice it was of him to fix the neighbor's lawn mower yesterday. He'll start to bluster, puff out his chest, and forget all about chastising you. Then he'll agree it was nice of him. It was damn fine, as a matter of fact. And, during dinner, he'll regale you with the tale of his virtuous deed. It's that attention thing.

If You Love One—Leo Woman

Just put on your résumé that you worked for Martha Stewart. That's more valuable than all the overtime I could pay you.

MARTHA STEWART (AUGUST 3)

She's loyal, steadfast, and true. Her animal magnetism is tangible whether she's wearing blue jeans or a business suit. The Leo woman seeks a mate who is attentive, romantic, and hardworking. She's sentimental, fun loving, and her view of life is refreshingly simple. "All ways here are the queen's ways." This line from *Alice's Adventures in Wonderland* describes, with near-perfection, Leo woman's personality. Remember this, and chances are you two will get along fine. If you refuse to acknowledge her omnipresence, remember this warning. No matter how quiet or charming your Lioness appears on the surface, her metaphorical claws are just as sharp as her four-legged sister roaming the plains of Africa.

She's more hussy than Highness. This woman carves just as many notches on her headboard as her male counterpart does, and is the one woman in the Universe who writes her own phone number on the locker-room wall. She loves the mirror as much as Libra does and lives for luxury, as does Capricorn. The difference is, her mirrors are guilt-edged and line her bedroom walls. Whereas a lady Goat will dress expensively but understated, the Lioness prefers an Aries Bob Mackie knockoff she got on sale. Her motto is, "If you've got it, flaunt it. If you don't, fake it."

This is also true in the bedroom. She may play the sex kitten, but a Leo woman is more interested in power than porno. If you are good-looking, have money to burn, are a power player, or can introduce her to someone who is, she'll drape herself over your bed or the backseat of your Lincoln just long enough to test whether you know the difference between a Radiant-cut and a Princess-cut. If you jokingly say, "Hairstyle," expect a look that could melt sand into glass. If you're serious, you're probably an Aquarius.

In love, she expects weekly flowers, daily phone calls, and a romantic getaway at least once a month. Unless you are rich, you'd better start applying for a low-interest second mortgage if you don't want to lose her to a Capricorn in Gucci loafers. She'll probably work, but will spend her salary on day spas, makeovers, and the latest fad diet.

The female Lion appreciates humor. Hers. She laughs at her own jokes and when at full throttle, can be as loud as Leo Lucille Ball. Except you won't be able to turn down her sound, and she won't shut up until she's ready. Those blasé wisecracks she dispenses at dinner seem natural and off-the-cuff. Actually, she spent three hours on the Internet sorting spam this afternoon.

Leo Mae West is a classic example of the archetypical female Lion. West's outrageous style and nonstop sexual innuendo were her trademarks. Only a Leo would have the brass to write, produce, and star in a play called *Sex* in 1925. She became notorious for one-liners such as, "I'm a girl who lost her reputation and never missed it," and "When I'm good, I'm very good, but when I'm bad, I'm better!" She was smart, sly, and way ahead of her time.

True to her over-the-top Leonine character, West pushed her luck too long and too hard. At eighty-five she still wore her hair cascading over her shoulders, although it looked more like a damp mop than a silky mane. Her makeup was garish and she propped herself up on the arms of sweating body-builders young enough to be her grandkids. West had become a caricature. The hooker with a heart of gold turned into a hag who refused to relinquish the spotlight.

Yours won't be quite as vain, but will demand lots of attention. Whether she's quiet and regal, or slinky and untamed, a Leo woman is as high-maintenance as they come.

If You Are One-Born Rotten

I have never loved another person the way I love myself.

Mae West (August 17)

Anywhere you go, you command attention. That's because you are usually carrying a gun. You vie with Aries for the Most Obnoxious Human award and pick arguments in sports bars just to show everyone who's boss.

You are first to aid friends and family in times of need and just as quick to announce to the world how good hearted you were to offer assistance. You assume control of every situation where more than one person is gathered. In an elevator you position yourself next to the door and push the floor buttons. At the grocery store you instruct the bag boy how to pack the sack.

Your idea of a good career is any profession in which your title is longer than your business card. Leo is the sign of the grade-school teacher, TV wrestler, karaoke champ, and floating crap game organizer. Lions also make good hair stylists, actors, and conga line leaders.

You don't do solitude. Instead, you head for the nearest party, arriving fashionably late so you can sweep into the room offering your fingertips and air kisses to your loyal fans as you head to the center of the action. Your nature is so theatrical that you can't bear the thought of being just one of the crowd and you will stand on your head, or someone else's back, to grab the spotlight.

Your home is your castle, where you rule by intimidation. You spend your evenings scolding your family, yelling at the dog, and hanging up on your mother. Your temper is like a solar flare. It flashes out, singeing the ears of the hapless person who dared to disagree, then dissipates just as quickly. Because you have selective memory, you think you are calm, cool, and collected and will beat the hell out of anyone who disagrees.

In romance you have all the finesse of a sailor returning from a twelve-month cruise. You'll go home with anyone who offers to buy you a six-dollar beer and tells you that you have great hair. The next day, you bore your friends with tales of sexual conquest that everyone knows are lies. What you don't know is that, secretly, everyone hopes you get eaten by a crocodile.

Your checking account serves as a clearinghouse between your paycheck and creditors, and you've filed for bankruptcy so often you're banned from using credit cards until 2052. Your favorite game is Follow the Leader, with you at the head of the group. But, instead of Captain Courageous, you are more like the captain of the *Titanic*. You never know where you are going and invariably lead everyone to disaster.

In real life, John Wayne was a Gemini. However, every role he ever played was pure Leo. Always strong, sometimes arrogant, his characters always knew just what they wanted and just how to get it. So do you.

You are lively, sincere, and elegant. Your independent nature is most contented when you are fighting for a cause, or an underdog. However, since your vices can be as large as your virtues, you need to learn to redirect some of your powerful energy. Give your attention to others versus calling it to yourself. Focus on taking time to understand more and criticize less, and not a sign in the zodiac will be able to resist you. In the meantime, anyone who wants to wrestle with a Lion will soon find out that you are still King of the Jungle.

You walk over the Earth signs with no fear. One swipe of your powerful claws stops Taurus in its charging tracks. Virgo instinctively knows to defer to your regal bearing, and you verbally shake Capricorn by its hairy neck until it's limp with fear. You definitely have a feline taste for seafood, and one glimpse of a gleaming fang sends petulant Pisces diving for cover. Should a cracked Crab scuttle out to bite your paw, you snap it up for a tasty midafternoon snack. And sullen Scorpio's stinger can't deflate either your sunny disposition or your ego. The Air signs, Gemini, Aquarius, and Libra, simply can't ruffle your fur, no matter how hard they posture and blow. You and fellow Fire signs, Aries and Sagittarius, understand each other on a soul level, and, therefore, rarely have serious confrontations.

Yours is the philosophy of "Work hard, play hard." You believe in living life to the fullest and see no reason to let anyone tell you differently. You are totally independent and have the serendipitous fortune of often being in the right place at the right time. Let the rest of the world clip coupons and save for a rainy day. Years from now, when your old lovers and ex-friends are living off their pensions and eating two-for-one canned chili, you can generously use some of that million-dollar jackpot you hit in Vegas to send along a case of Beluga caviar and a magnum of Dom Perignon.

It's ALL Relative—The Leo Family

I didn't even have a television when I was growing up.

LAURA LEIGHTON (JULY 24)

Whether benevolent dictators or absolute rulers, Leo parents have laws, rules, and curfews. The earlier you understand this, the easier life in a Leo-ruled home will be. Mom won't tolerate any behavior that embarrasses her in public. A Leo dad probably invented the phrase "Children should be seen and not heard." Both will yell when they are angry, which is often. Neither will apologize. They love giving orders, so you might as well get used to it.

Your Leo parents expect you to defer to their judgment, obey without question, and take out the garbage with a smile. They won't like your friends, your hair, or your choice of cars. You will have tennis lessons, piano lessons, tap dance lessons, and gymnastics coaching under your belt by the time you reach first grade. Leo parents groom their children to be successful, whether they want to or not.

Leo toddlers are sunny, happy, and playful—as long as they have your undivided attention. And he will have it, one way or the other—either your laughter at his silly antics or your exasperation when he dumps the milk on the floor because you hugged his sister.

Leo teenagers drive too fast, party too late, and are generally rebellious. These are not the kids to leave in charge when you go away for the weekend, unless you carry heavy-duty liability insurance. As students, they are usually smart, but often lazy. *Indolent* is a better word because, like their jungle counterparts, young human Lions like to sleep late, then wander around aimlessly, sniffing out their next adventure. Start taming yours the day he or she is born.

Leo siblings are boring show-offs. As toddlers they scream if you ignore them. As teens, they pout if you ignore them. They will order you around, compete for your parents' affections, and disappear when it's time to do the dishes. They will ask you to do their homework because they have a date, and bet you their allowance they can sneak out of the house at midnight without Mom or Dad waking up. It's a safe bet, but collecting is another matter.

How do you survive in a home that's more circus than serene? Easy. The earlier you understand that you can charm, flatter, or whine anything you want out of any of your Leo relatives, the more fun you will have.

Office Party—Bitches, Snitches, and the Chronically Inert

There is a certain combination of anarchy and discipline in the way I work.

ROBERT DE NIRO (AUGUST 17)

A Lion is the most dominant, arrogant, and self-centered boss in the Universe. He won't hesitate to use every trick in the book, or the boardroom, to get his way.

This boss will ask you to rewrite the cost-savings plan, and after you stay up all night doing so, will tell his boss *he* stayed up all night. To make matters worse, his boss will let him take off the afternoon to get some rest.

His office will be decorated with statues of African fertility gods and a leather couch for those power naps he takes while you go without lunch. When he awakes, he'll delegate everything on his desk, then go golfing since he has nothing to do.

She sees you as one of her subjects and, therefore, wastes little time in either small talk or pleasantries. The most you will get from her is a question of whether or not you like her new suit or the ten-carat diamond ring she charged on her credit card.

Your Leo coworkers are too busy trying to win the Employee of the Year award than to try for your job. He or she will regularly make the rounds of the company, just like a Lion makes rounds of his hunting ground. The prey they scope out are, in order, potential lovers, the bulletin board to hunt for bargains, and the lunch counter for a double cheeseburger, chocolate malt, and curly fries. Their work will collect in a box under the desk until the boss asks for the assignment that was due a week ago. Then your Leo cubicle-mate will simply lie that she distinctly remembers asking you to do it because she was too busy.

Irk a Lion by refusing to bow. Be pleasant but distant. Remain calm at all times and try not to jump when one sneaks up behind you. Eat lunch from the stash of snacks she keeps in her desk. Taking away his toys is another way to make one yowl. Tell him the boss said no more nudie calendars and whoopee cushions. That's sure to keep him or her making the rounds to the supervisor, the manager, and the director of personnel, rebelling, yelling, and, eventually, getting fired themselves.

Can't We ALL Get Along?

Short of using a whip and a chair, how do you tame the king of beasts? Easy. A little flattery gets you everything.

Flamboyant Lions

Being ruled by the Sun gives every Leo a natural flair for drama and an instinctive talent for getting attention. This is the most public sign in the zodiac. As such, Lions are very concerned with their image, and the idea of losing the respect of those they admire is unthinkable. They are also naturally playful, outspoken, and like to tell jokes. This combination of regal and ribald is sometimes hard for them to manage. Especially at the office Christmas party. Next time yours gets a little too slaphappy, or wants to wear a yellow velvet jumpsuit, cut to the naval: appeal to her dignified side.

To accomplish this goal, first compliment, then suggest. For instance, tell her the roast beef sandwich she made at lunch was superb. Then remind her that the president of the company is going to be at the party, and that a more reserved outfit might be best. Her eyes are so expressive, what about the dress that matches them? And so on . . . until she's decided that she should wear her gray silk and matching pearls, because a good first impression is so important.

Bossy Lions

All Leos feel their home is their castle. They don't like having their opinions questioned or their decisions second-guessed. They are self-assured and comfortable being boss. The problems start when they forget that other people's wishes and opinions are as important as their own, and they attempt to use force, fear, or just plain bratty behavior to get their way.

Since all wild things like a roaring good fight, save yourself laryngitis by appealing to your Lion's sense of generosity and vanity. A little TLC goes a long way with Leo. Tell yours how wise, witty, and wonderful he or she is, and when his or her eyes start to glitter, simply ask for what you want. Lions are big hearted and love being charitable. And you'll love knowing how easy it is to get your way.

Spendthrift Leos

The people who designed those racks of impulse buys next to the checkout stand must have had the Leonine personality in mind. Leos are not good negotiators. They see something they want and they grab it on the spur of the moment, then often regret their decision.

To save yourself the misery of having a living room–size leopard-skin rug, velvet paintings of Elvis, King of the Capricorns, hanging in the bedroom, or a garage full of garish furniture and gilded knickknacks, try to go shopping with yours as much as possible. At the swap meet, remind him that if he forgoes the plastic flamingos for the yard, he could buy the set of Virgo Buddy Holly records you found at the next table. He'll love that you were thinking of him (as usual) and you'll love the fact that you won't have to face the neighbors (again).

Flirty Leos

The legend that all Leos are self-indulgent, egotistical, shallow, and faithless couldn't be further from the truth. They are the Universe's biggest flirts because they genuinely like the opposite sex. You will never change that, but you will also rarely have to worry about yours straying. Lions are homebodies at heart. They feel secure in their own environment, where they are loved and respected for themselves. Keep romance alive with an active social calendar, pet them, pamper them, and remember that a little flattery goes a long way. In return, you will have a tender, gentle lover who will never forget your birthday or anniversary. Just like their jungle cousins, Lions mate for life.

Quick Tips for Emergencies

- ♌ Lions need respect.
- ♌ Usually, their roar is sharper than their claws.
- ♌ Attention and flattery keeps your Lion purring.
- ♌ One expensive gift is better than lots of little nothings.
- ♌ Gaslight them by ignoring their roaring.

Jungle Cats

Yasser Arafat
Fidel Castro
Amy Fisher
Carl Jung
David Koresh
Monica Lewinsky
Madonna
Slobodan Milosevic
Phyllis Schlafly
Danielle Steel

Chapter Seven

Virgo

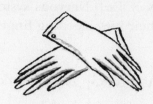

August 23–September 22

EverLasting Know-It-ALLs Need Love, Too

Element: Earth. Virgo Earth is a solid parcel of common soil that provides everything you need in a predictable manner—as predictable as Bermuda grass. Mow it, water it, mow it, water it.

Quality: Mutable. Virgo moods swing from nitpicker, to crank, to critic.

Symbol: The Virgin. In your dreams and their minds.

Ruler: Mercury, the god of Telling It Like It Is . . . whether or not you want to hear it.

Favorite Pastime: Worrying.

Favorite Book: *1001 Steps to Total Organization.*

Role Model: Felix Unger.

Dream Job: Closet organizer.

Key Phrase: "It won't work that way."

Body Part: Nervous system. You can always spot a Virgo by their raw, bleeding fingernails.

Approach with Caution

Virgo, the sixth sign of the zodiac, lives in the House of Service and Health. Tactful astrology depicts Virgo as a modest, practical peach of a person who is superbly logical, discriminating, and meticulous. A more accurate description might reveal an anal, subjective, self-absorbed fussbudget who is critical, sanctimonious, and cheap.

Virgo is ruled by Mercury, the same breezy character that rules pesky Gemini. However, in Virgo, Mercury's mischievous, lighthearted nature is trapped in Earth, where it becomes critical and irritable. Virgos would like to be as unstructured as cousin Gemini, but their feet are stuck firmly in the ground. Virgins sweat the small stuff. These folks are compelled to heal the sick, save the sinful, and correct everyone else's spelling. They dispense unsolicited advice with all the authority of a second-grade teacher, with about as much insight.

Virgo's are deliberate, not spontaneous. They are so busy trying to perfect everyone else that they have lost sight of their own flawed natures. Of all the signs, Virgo is the least likely to admit a mistake. Born with the nothing's-ever-good-enough gene has made them unable to relax and enjoy life's surprises. Bring your lunch, and dinner, if you dare to argue with one, because they will never admit they are wrong. Prove a Virgin wrong and he, or she, will say, "Oh, I didn't realize that. Well, that changes the whole perspective . . . now, if you had only explained that to me at the beginning."

If You Love One–Virgo Man

I'm not afraid to let people know that I'm kind of an idiot.

TERRY BRADSHAW (SEPTEMBER 2)

He's faithful, thoughtful, and cool-headed during a crisis. A Virgo man will be home in time for dinner, help you balance the checkbook, and help raise the children. Whether he's as sexy as Sean Connery, or as silly as Peter Sellers, he will always be by your side. He's conscientious, capable, thrifty, kind, and loyal. Sounds like a real Boy Scout, doesn't he? Well, he is—the bargain basement version.

Life with a male Virgin is like being pushed into traffic when you don't want to cross the street. Born with a superior attitude and an eye for improving everything except his own conduct, he is as relentless with his fault-finding as a pit bull locked onto a mailman's leg, and just as unsympathetic.

At his worst, he's a classic chauvinist, dismissing what he doesn't believe and believing only what's convenient to his point of view. His one talent for conversation is a nonstop string of criticisms about every facet of your existence, from the way you wear your hair to your coupon-clipping ability. And he won't hesitate to insult your intelligence by demonstrating just how to accomplish either task.

At his best, he has the kind of predictability that will give you sleeping sickness. He'll expect dinner promptly at six, where you will exchange news of the day's events. Then he'll spend an hour with the children, who will go to bed exactly at eight. Next comes an hour of telling you how to improve your housekeeping abilities. Finally, he'll retire to his home office where he'll spend the rest of the evening mumbling over the bills or developing a plan for your self-improvement.

His character is purely idiosyncratic. Every Virgo has his own peculiar thought process and just as peculiar speech pattern. Many self-made Virgo millionaires are unable to utter a sensible statement.

Throughout his career, legendary Hollywood producer Virgo Samuel Goldwyn adamantly refused to compromise his search for the finest talent, directors, screenwriters, and technical crews. You can't argue with perfection, and The Goldwyn Touch set a standard of excellence that has been seldom, if ever, matched. Sam also had an unmatched Virgo talent for trying to act superior and coming off as a total goofball.

When his secretary asked for permission to destroy files over ten years old, Goldwyn said, "Yes, but keep copies." He's also credited with such gems as, "Give me a couple of years, and I'll make that actress an overnight success," "If I look confused, it's because I'm thinking," and "True. I've been a long time making up my mind, but now I'm giving you a definite answer . . . maybe."

Argue with yours, and he'll stare at you as if you've just lost your mind, for he can't believe you dared to disagree. Then he will repeat, word by word, the conversation, question, or disagreement that led you to throw the toaster at his head. Soon, you will feel as if ants were crawling through your brain and will apologize just to shut him up.

You can take comfort in the knowledge that if you are determined to force his hand, you can send him to bed with a stomachache. The fact that he's pretending to be ill, and he knows you know it, makes no difference. A male Virgo will feign anything from a headache to a heart attack if he feels cornered. He's as loath to confront a situation as is his opposite, Pisces, but where Pisces fears confrontation itself, Virgo fears facing any unpleasantries about himself. Of course, he will expect you to rush to his side with chicken soup and spoon-feed him. If he can't control you with his superiority, he'll try to by appearing helpless.

He may appear to be calm, cool, and collected on the outside, but on the inside he's pure Felix Unger. The effeminate, priggish, germ-phobic half of the Odd Couple is a classic example of the Virgo male. In his unyielding efforts to save slob Oscar from his boorish ways, Felix totally lost sight of his own obnoxious behavior. His deodorant-spraying, dust-rag-flapping, nonstop derision of Oscar's lifestyle, coupled with his melodramatic hypochondria, is totally Virgo.

If you want romance and love songs, choose any other sign (except Capricorn), because you won't find it with this man. Serve him dinner by candlelight and he'll complain he can't see what he's eating. He'll talk a lot about sex and isn't above leering at the nearest pretty face. However, he's really not into promiscuity, even the legal kind, except on Wednesday and Saturday nights, unless it's tax season, then revise that schedule to Saturday from 9 to 9:15. He's so methodical that you can put a cake in the oven and be assured that his buzzer will go off five minutes before the kitchen timer.

A Virgo man is nervous, nitpicky, and as selfish as a spinster guarding her assets. Emotional scenes baffle and alarm him because he fears losing control. Unless, of course, he plans to lose control, and even then he will try to orchestrate the outcome. Like Mr. Spock, too much unbridled passion makes his brain melt.

If You Love One—Virgo Woman

I don't like to think of myself as neurotic, but I do like things clean!

BARBARA EDEN (AUGUST 23)

The Virgo woman is kind, caring, and very real. Her exterior may be calm, but her feelings are delicate and she seeks a mate who is intelligent, considerate, and warm-hearted. She believes in true love and is discriminating enough to wait until she finds it. That's why there are so many Virgo old maids.

Queen Elizabeth I, the Virgin Queen, reigned alone as England's monarch for forty-four years. The marriage of a queen regent was extremely complicated, and Elizabeth did not want to make an unpopular match. At least that's history's version. True to her perfectionist Virgo nature, Good Queen Bess marched suitors from around the world in and out of her court for twenty-five years, eliminating each one for various and sundry reasons. They either were the wrong religion, not intelligent, too poor, too political, not powerful, or too powerful. Elizabeth nitpicked her way to spinsterhood as only a female Virgo can.

If you manage to survive your Virgin's checklist of partnership virtues (and she has a long one), you will soon find that living with a Virgo female is like being enrolled for life in the School of Unattainable Perfection.

She's critical. A female Virgin will analyze and critique everything from your choice of cars to the way you slice the Thanksgiving turkey. She will count the number of peas you eat and lay a neat pile of vitamins beside your water glass. She will expect you to use the proper fork; a crumpled napkin tossed in the middle of your bread-polished plate will send her into a nervous fit. She's a creature of habit. Tell this woman you will arrive at eight, and you had better be on time, or five minutes early. One minute late is inexcusable.

To her, a perfect weekend consists of nagging the family into cleaning the closets or replanting the garden while she criticizes every move, then later makes herself sick by redoing everything. Although she considers herself well organized and tidy, your home will always look as if pirates have just ransacked it. That's because she's too busy making her to-do list to do anything.

When angry, she is fussy and inflexible. The best thing to do is apologize, even if you have no idea what set her off. Otherwise you will suffer a garrulous scolding that will make you wish she'd just had your ass dragged over a bed of hot coals.

As a love object, think of her as a fortress to which you are about to lay siege. Launch your first attack with a show of brainpower and gift her with a couple of thought-provoking books.

Next, spit-shine your shoes, buy a new shirt and some crisp-smelling cologne. *Clean* is a holy word to a Virgo female and you'll knock a chink in her armor with a pristine appearance.

Finally, when you are knocking on the door of Virgin-Heaven, be patient. A Virgo woman is full of passion—once you get through the terrycloth robe, nightgown, socks, Vicks, and cold cream.

If You Are One-Born Rotten

Don't get mad, get even.

Joseph Kennedy (September 6)

You have one belief. Everyone in life is beneath you. There isn't an idea that you can't improve upon, or a person you can't whip into shape. You may pride yourself on being a discriminating perfectionist, but everyone else sees you as a royal pain in the ass. You are very intelligent, but can't make any practical use of your knowledge, so you end up spouting platitudes and pumping gas.

You have Forest for the Trees Syndrome. You are so bogged down in the excruciating minutiae of daily life that you let the world, and your dreams, pass by. But that's OK with you, since it gives you a reason to blame your faults on every one but yourself.

Yours is the sign of the scribe, prosecuting attorney, mimic, despot, and anything with *critic* in the title. Virgos make excellent bureaucrats because they love to make people stand for hours in lines that go nowhere.

You spend your life moving your metaphorical piles of dirty laundry from one side of your psyche to the other without resolving anything. However, this is fine with you because it gives you something to do on Saturday night besides rearranging your medicine cabinet.

You are so concerned with your health that you rattle when

you walk from all the pill bottles jiggling in your pocket or purse. Your home serves as a satellite pharmacy for the neighborhood and you delight in dispensing the latest holistic advice on every ailment from boils to constipation. You are the type of patient who hounds your doctor for double prescriptions, just to be prepared.

Your favorite game is Mountains out of Molehills, and you obsess over things that will never happen. You spend hours worrying whether or not you should use milk that's one day past its pull date and if your tires have enough air to get you to your next dentist appointment. You are the only sign in the zodiac that looks forward to a tooth cleaning. You have more systems for coping with life than the IRS has for tracking down tax dodgers.

In love, you are as romantic as a top sergeant drilling the troops. You expect your lover to adhere to your timetable and preferences and balk at any variation. After you invariably get dumped, you cry for about five minutes, then decide that he, or she, wasn't good enough for you anyway and grab the nearest good book to soothe yourself. When you do get the urge to merge, you usually make the wrong choice, because you've been so picky in the past that you suddenly find yourself on the downside of sexy and grab the first person you can clutch in your impeccably manicured little hands.

You also have exceptional self-discipline and your will is so strong that you can easily make all your dreams come true. You are often misjudged because of your perfectionist attitude. Truth is you never expect more of others than that which you are willing to give. You are sympathetic and generous and have a genuine desire to help people do their best. But you need to cultivate more patience and less assumption that your opinion is always either correct or sought. Instead of scattering your energy trying to control the world, learn to listen first, then take aim with a few well-chosen barbs, and there isn't a sign in the Universe you can't outwit.

When Leo wants a war, you eloquently prove that the

tongue is mightier than the roar. Your refusal to waste your energy on the childish antics of Aries or Sagittarius drives both of these zodiacal clowns to self-destruction. You can freeze Water signs Cancer, Scorpio, and Pisces in their emotion-sodden tracks with one or two well-chosen observations about their self-delusional natures. Gemini and Aquarius will quickly realize that their impudent sarcasm is no match for your cool self-assurance. And self-indulgent Libra simply can't measure up to your standards. You and fellow Earth signs Taurus and Capricorn understand each other on a soul level and, therefore, rarely have serious confrontations.

Your philosophy is "A time and place for everything." You believe in moral principle and old-fashioned family values. Let everyone else run through life in a slapdash, offhanded sort of way. You are too busy making that impossible dream come true, one organized step at a time. Years from now when your enemies are sucking baby food from a bendable straw, you will cheerfully send them each a case of strained peas, special delivery, from your private island somewhere in the South Pacific.

It's ALL Relative—The Virgo Family

Instead of those harsh cleansers, I use baking soda. Cleans every bit as good. It's cheaper. Baking soda's dirt-cheap.

ED BEGLEY, JR. (SEPTEMBER 16)

Being raised in a Virgo-ruled home is like living in a benign sort of boot camp. Instead of teddy bears, your first toys will be a miniature calculator with brightly colored keys and a piggy bank that snorts when you "feed" it coins. Before you learn the alphabet, you will learn the virtue of saving pennies. And as soon as you can walk to the laundry room, you'll be taught that cleanliness is next to Godliness.

Virgo parents will watch you like a hawk watches a gopher.

And will just as instantly swoop down to correct a word or deed. Mom will white-glove your room on a daily basis and won't be satisfied until she's crawled into the darkest corner of your closet and dug out a dust bunny to hold under your nose.

Dad will design a mini–work space in the corner of his home office, where you can have the fun of learning how to play the stock market instead of Sega. You will learn the value of two-for-one specials and how to hang the toilet paper so it pulls from under versus over, thus making the roll last longer. You'll have books instead of balls and watch *Sesame Street* instead of *Scooby-Doo.*

Your Virgo baby will learn to tie her shoes, dress herself, and have a vocabulary to rival yours by the time she's three. Her biggest desire is to help you clean house, and this is one child, male or female, who you will rarely have to tell to tidy up her room.

Virgo kids smile a lot, even when they stoutly refuse to do what you are yelling at them to do. Virgins are born set in their ways, and there is little or nothing you can do to change them.

As teens, they manipulate by frequent sighing and theatrical posturing. She will tell you that she would like to borrow your car to take a poor, crippled friend to the movies Friday night. Sounds selfless, but in reality the friend is a pal who twisted her ankle climbing out the bedroom window to meet her boyfriend, and your kid is picking them both up on her way to her steady's house for a party.

Virgo siblings paint a large stripe down the center of your shared bedroom and tell you never to set foot on their side. They will constantly grump about everything from Mom's cooking to Dad's hobbies, act superior in front of your friends, and make fun of them behind their backs. You seldom argue, though. By the time you both learned to talk, you learned to tune out and just go ahead and do what you pleased.

So how do you have any fun in a family full of nitpicking perfectionists? Simple. Since your Virgo family members are so firmly entrenched in their respective ruts and hate any changes in the daily routine, you can cheerfully volunteer to run those last-minute errands. It will allow you a breath of fresh air. Oh, and don't forget your piggy bank. You may have quit feeding it pennies years ago, but your thrifty parents have made it fat with enough greenbacks to pay for your first year in college.

Office Party—Bitches, Snitches, and the Chronically Inert

> *If I didn't start painting, I would have raised chickens.*
> GRANDMA MOSES (SEPTEMBER 7)

A Virgo boss has two basic rules: Don't make any mistakes of your own and never point out his. If you can keep these straight, you'll stand a fair chance of keeping your job for a reasonable length of time. That is, if you can stand working for a Virgin.

Virgo bosses are perfectionists. They are as judgmental as Taurus, fastidious as Leo, and will constantly evaluate your appearance, performance, and popularity with your coworkers, none of which will measure up to their picayune standards. They will subject you to endless suggestions and pointed comments designed to mold you into the perfect employee.

A Virgo in an executive position is usually in over his or her head, which can exacerbate a penchant for micromanagement. Lieutenant William Bligh, whose horrid lists of rules and punishments drove Libra Fletcher Christian and the crew to mutiny on the *Bounty,* neatly fits this profile. Historians described Bligh as "overbearing, self-righteous, and insensitive to the problems and feelings of others." Bligh also had some nonspecific illness that kept him in his quarters much of the time, on both the *Bounty*'s and successive voyages, which could have been typical Virgin nervous indigestion.

Your boss may not be as mean, but he will need you to field

questions and put out the office fires. He will be too busy washing down his fingernails with Pepto-Bismol because all that responsibility has given him an ulcer.

He is a creature of habit, so expect yours to eat lunch at the same time each day and to have as many standing appointments and regular meetings scheduled as possible. Either sex will also not hesitate to resort to the lowest tactics of blackmail and manipulation to get ahead.

Virgo Lyndon B. Johnson once said, "I never trust a man unless I've got his pecker in my pocket." Johnson was known for the unremitting pressure he put upon people whose support he needed. He once discovered that a married colleague, whose vote he needed to pass a bill, was having an affair. First Johnson called the man, trying to garner his vote. When that didn't work, he sent the congressman's wife a dozen roses, then called her to invite the couple to the White House for lunch. The subtle threat worked and LBJ got his vote.

Your Virgo boss will expect you to keep her pencils sharpened and her messages in chronological order. She will rewrite your letters, tell you to organize your messy desk, and send you home to change clothes should you spill a drop of coffee on your sleeve. She will not be interested in your personal problems, although she will freely tell you all of hers in boring detail.

Virgo coworkers have the neatest desks in the office. That's because they spend all their time either organizing their paperwork into tidy, untouched piles or calling in sick because they have too much to do.

If a Virgo sets her sights on your job, it's probably because he, or she, thinks that you do less work and get paid more money, or you have the authority to delegate work to the rest of the staff. She will not hesitate to try to discredit you with your other coworkers or blatantly tell the boss how she could do your job better.

To foil this backstabber, simply confront her with the evidence that your colleagues will be happy to corroborate and tell her that if she doesn't lay off, you are going to show the boss where she's hidden the last two weeks' worth of unposted sales figures.

To irk the Virgo in the next cubicle, come in early and rearrange his desktop. Switch the stapler to the phone side, and the phone to the credenza. Move the stack of invoices to the left and the envelopes to the right. Or, if you want to be less ornery and more subtle, just tweak the lists, schedules, pictures, and inspirational clichés he has tacked to his space divider until they are a hairsbreadth off center. Then sit back and listen to the muffled laughter of the whole office as Mr. Virgo spends the rest of the day getting organized.

Can't We All Get Along?

How is it possible to share space with the most anal creature on Earth and live to tell the tale? Simple, once you know the system.

Hypercritical Virgins

There's no getting around it, Virgo is the sign of the perfectionist, and all Virgins are nitpickers. However, most of their criticism is self-directed. When they feel they've failed to live up to the exacting personal standards they've set for themselves, then they turn their critical eye outward.

When yours starts carping, a little understanding goes a long way. Praise works wonders for all ages and both sexes. So does eating on time, leaving the mail in its proper place, and having a clean set of their favorite old clothes ready to slip into when they get home. Virgos prefer to talk about their troubles, so be prepared to listen sympathetically as you massage their tired feet and throbbing temples.

Hypochondriac Virgins

Part of the care and feeding of a Virgo includes dealing with an occasional bout of psychosomatic stomach flu, allergies, or headache. Virgos realize they make themselves sick, but still can't help feeling ill. They also pretend to be sick in order to avoid confrontation.

To keep yours as healthy and stressfree as possible, include plenty of fresh, organic fruits and vegetables, whole grains, purified water, and fish in their diets. Vitamin supplements help, as does lavender in the bath and at the bedside. Home-made soup, spoonfed by you, is a downright miraculous cure.

Freaked-Out Virgins

All Virgos are slightly compulsive-obsessive and some are truly clinical. Virgos have so much Mercurial energy coursing through their brains that they constantly assess, process, and judge what to improve and what to pass by every waking moment. This makes them absentminded with respect to mundane chores. Their inner critic rears its ugly head at the most inopportune times, like when you are just about to board your flight for Hawaii, and they worry that they've forgotten to turn off the iron or lock the front door.

A little reassurance goes a long way. Tell your Virgo that you are positive everything was fine when you left and don't let them postpone your vacation to rush home and rattle the door. Offer to call a neighbor and if you do find out the house is on fire, forget it. You can collect the insurance when you get back.

Virgins in Need of a Romantic Boost

Virgins are not virginal. Neither are they sexless, clueless, or cold-hearted. They do not prefer reading books to getting laid and don't really post lovemaking schedules on the back of the closet door. Well, most don't.

They are reticent. Virgos build trust very slowly, and without trust you have no chance at winning either sex's heart.

After you are happily settled into a serious relationship, you can keep romance alive quite nicely.

First, be patient. Second, remember that Virgos are creatures of habit, so don't try for a quickie on the kitchen table, unless you've managed to incorporate it into one of the acceptable places your Virgin will surrender. Keep your body fit and your mind alert. Virgo appreciates intellect and doesn't like surprises. With a little kindness, an honest but gentle approach and lots of TLC, you and your Virgo will keep the home fires burning brightly.

Quick Tips for Emergencies

♍ Virgins need routine.

♍ Keep them calm with nutritious food and a back rub.

♍ Talking out frustrations helps prevent petulant criticism.

♍ Planning is key to getting your way.

♍ Gaslight them by rearranging their sock drawers.

Virgo Cranks and Critics

Tim Burton

Niles Crane

Albert DeSalvo (The Boston Strangler)

Dilbert

Elvira, Mistress of the Night

Michael Jackson

Paula Jones

Miss Manners (Judith Martin)

Paul Reubens, aka Pee-Wee Herman

Gene Simmons

Chapter Eight

Libra

September 23–October 22

Mirror, Mirror, on the Wall

Element: Air. Libra Air produces a constant droning in your ears. Libra's idea of rational discussion is that they discuss and you listen rationally. Eventually, you feel like your head is trapped within a beehive.

Quality: Cardinal. Libra is boss backbiter, belittler, and bimbo.

Symbol: The Scales. Off balance. Permanently tipped in Libra's favor. Swings both ways.

Ruler: Venus, the goddess of plastic surgeons and mirrored ceilings.

Favorite Pastime: Smirking.

Favorite Book: *How to Marry Yourself.*

Role Model: Barbie/Ken.

Dream Job: Devil's advocate.

Key Phrase: "On the other hand . . ."

Body Part: Kidneys, full of gravel from the teeth they grind at night to compensate for all that phony smiling during the day.

Approach with Caution

Libra's symbol, the Scales, represents life's continual balancing act. Libra lives in the Seventh House of Partnerships. Sugar-coated astrology tells us that Libras are harmonious, impartial, diplomatic peacemakers who seek truth, beauty, and the perfect mate. Truth is, beneath that cloying smile lives a self-indulgent, indecisive gold digger who has the personality of a leaf.

Libra is ruled by the bad-girl goddess, Venus. In Taurus, Venus bestows a greedy nature that craves possessions. In Libra, she bestows an endless hunger for perfection. Libras are never satisfied, with either themselves or you. Being one of the bossy Cardinal signs, Libras view dissent as a personal affront. They pout if you change the radio station. Libra's idea of peace and harmony is your total agreement with their philosophy of the moment.

Have some fun by telling yours that his or her horoscope disagrees with the fortune cookie they just read to you. That should send either gender straight for the aspirin and a cold washcloth.

Libras are subjective, not judicious. Their skewed sense of justice distorts their ability to accept any argument or opinion other than their own. Being born without the justice-is-blind gene has rendered them unable to remain truly impartial. Argue with one, and suffer a sudden explosion of rage. Prove your point, and vacillating Libra may verbally agree. Silently, he or she will never forgive you for being right.

If You Love One-Libra Man

I can resist anything . . . except temptation.

OSCAR WILDE (OCTOBER 16)

He's funny, charismatic, and oozes charm. His sense of style is impeccable and his lively, friendly personality puts him at the top of everyone's A-list. A Libra male is an idealistic dreamer who believes in world peace and fair play. He will take you to the most expensive restaurant in town, declare his adoration in front of the smiling patrons, and drop to one knee to propose. Before you exclaim, "Yes, my darling," make sure he's still looking at you. By the time he's slipped the engagement ring on your finger, he will have spotted his next conquest walking toward the bar.

A Libra man is perfectly capable of marrying you on Saturday and starting his next string of affairs on Sunday. He's fickle, inconsistent, and constantly on the prowl. Never mind Aries or Gemini. When it comes to love, the male Libra is as flaky as a used car salesman sniffing out his next sucker deal.

He's shallow. You may start thinking of a future together after a couple of rounds of his polished sexual prowess. However, to him, *future* is defined as until tomorrow morning, when he'll most likely forget your name before he finishes flossing his dazzling white teeth.

He's superficial. A Libra man prefers beauty to substance and expects to be blindsided by the emotion of perfect love. Oh, you'll hear bells ring, but, after the honeymoon, those harmonious chimes quickly turn to death knells. He doesn't want a real woman who will jar him out of his escapist daydreaming into a world of house payments and crying children. He wants a Barbie doll to cook, clean, and entertain his endless procession of casual friends.

He's not into anger. Pick a fight with him, and you'll get a half-hearted argument. Usually, he will verbally dodge, sidestep, and try to distract you from the original issue with all the nimbleness of a Capricorn skipping out on his alimony payments. Contrary to venting his anger, he will drive you to vent yours.

At best, he's an indecisive bumbler who's so easily distracted that he'll get sidetracked into spending the day at the races with a friend he met in the supermarket while you and the kids wait for dinner. Or he'll come home empty-handed from the paint store because he couldn't decide which shade of green to buy for the hothouse.

At worst, he's king of the lounge lizards. The seventies should be renamed the Decade of Libra Man. Wizened Lotharios from this era still have their blue polyester leisure suits, gold chains, pinkie rings, and an original bottle of Hai Karate. The modern versions wear leather vests over bare chests and strut like peacocks down the middle of the dance floor during the band's break, hoping every eye is turned in their direction.

He's a master of double-speak. Think of Libra Oliver North's statement, "I was provided with additional input that was radically different from the truth. I assisted in furthering that version." Ollie is the Libra poster child. The only thing this guy will spend hours rationalizing is his bad behavior.

He's also self-obsessed. Libra Timothy Leary used all of his formidable intelligence and personal magnetism to force the world to agree that his endless quest for a bigger high was actually the key to brave new worlds. When faced with the inevitable opposition, Leary reacted in typical Libra fashion. He devised an entire thought system to detract from his self-indulgence. In his mind, the rest of the world made a terrible error in judgment by not embracing his philosophy. And that issue was more important to his Libra soul than proving that the path to God was sprinkled with LSD and magic mushrooms.

Mr. Scaly has a give-and-take nature. You give. He takes. He will expect you to flatter his ego, coo as he preens, and help him pick the tie that best matches his eyes as he prepares for a night out with his friends. You, on the other hand, must never depress him with tedious details such as an overdrawn bank account or a leaky roof. Whether his dimpled good looks outweigh his self-serving ego is your decision.

If You Love One-Libra Woman

Everyone should have enough money to get plastic surgery.
BEVERLY JOHNSON (OCTOBER 13)

She is the sweetheart of the zodiac. Discriminating, thoughtful, romantic, and fair minded, lovely Libra's main objective is harmony and a meaningful relationship. She is warm, sensual, and feminine, and you will have to compete with several other ardent suitors for her delicate hand. If you're lucky, someone else will win it. If you thought Snow White's wicked stepmother was vain, jealous, and in love with her mirror, you've never fought a female Libra for a spot in the bathroom.

Along with Venus' smile, she's inherited a goddess's love of excess. A Libra female brandishes her credit card like a lethal weapon. God help you if it's rained for three days, or the cat coughed up a hairball on the bathroom rug. Nothing chases away this woman's blues like an afternoon of power shopping.

She never weighs the pros and cons of anything other than when is the best time for her next facial. It's not that she is stupid; it's just that a logical thought rarely makes it through the hairspray to her brain. By the time she's sixty, she'll more than likely be silicone from the ankles up. And, her decision-making skills are confined to turning in a circle three times and spitting over her left shoulder.

Just like her emotional structure, her famous taste for decorating is totally lopsided. She will live monk-style, with no furniture and a grass mat on the floor, or her home will look like the Smithsonian, crammed from floor to ceiling with every garish piece of "art" she can drag home. The latter thinks any uncovered wallspace is a mortal sin. The former hasn't a clue so assumes less is more, and none is better than less. Both, however, will not hesitate to tell you what's wrong with your color scheme, furniture selection, or that Ming vase in the entry—the one that, she thinks, came from Super K.

Super-Libra Emily Post was America's etiquette guru for forty years. Post instructed the nation on the proper way to set a table, serve and eat a nine-course meal, write a thank-you note, decline or accept an invitation, and throw a wedding or a funeral. But in classic vacillating Libra style, Post continually revised her definition of "good manners" to fit our changing society.

The female Libra craves attention, is usually promiscuous, and won't care whether you are an in-law, outlaw, married, or on parole, as long as you are cute and know how to dance.

At the tender age of sixteen, Bonnie Parker decided her life was boring and eloped with one of the hometown bad boys. Soon after, her husband went to jail for petty theft. Enter Aries Clyde Barrow, an older and slicker version of the small-time hick she'd married. Bonnie instantly bonded to his charm and daring—and just as instantly forgot her jailed spouse. The fact that every cop in three states was on their trail made no difference; Clyde fit her Libra ideal. He worshipped at her dainty feet and when the money ran out, robbed another bank to buy her a new dress.

"We" is the Libra female's favorite word. In romance, she moves as fast as a starved hyena closing in on a limping wildebeest. Offer her a cup of coffee, and she'll think you are after a date. Take her on a date, and she'll plan the wedding. Marry her, and she will make a tender and affectionate lover, for about a week. Then she will present you with her Rules of Use list. For example: You must be willing to help around the house. You must not under any circumstances use her towel or her bathroom. The longer you stick around, the longer the list gets, finally including your sexual behavior.

She will cling to you long after you've moved out, even if

parting was her idea. She's not pining. She wants to assure herself that you are suffering and will try to exercise her power to call you on a moment's notice for a quickie. If you are fool enough to fall for this and expect any tenderness afterward, or perhaps reconciliation, forget it. By the time you get dressed and back to your place, Ms. Libra will be hot on the scent of her next kill.

If You Are One-Born Rotten

Forget what you need and only think about what you desire.
DONNA KARAN (OCTOBER 2)

Your sole purpose in life is to be right all the time, and you constantly change your mind in order to ensure that fact. You have strong opinions that you always change in the face of disapproval. Since you never act on any of your endless declarations, your friends and family quickly learn that your advice is worthless and ignore it, and you.

Your much-touted intellect is merely an inborn talent for knowing fifty ways to say "On the other hand." This endless hemming and hawing is actually an avoidance mechanism designed to protect you from choosing sides or taking action. Libras flee from decision-making faster than a Sagittarius from a commitment ceremony.

You hate vulgar shouting matches and sordid emotional scenes, unless you are the one losing control. Even when angry, you can't act decisively. You deliberate over all the actions you could take and wonder whether you should ignore the incident or go postal. By the time you decide, the person you are mad at has forgotten you exist and moved to Bolivia.

You are the most social sign in the zodiac and use any excuse to party. That's because without an audience, you bore yourself to sleep. You can, however, intuitively sense when someone needs help. This is extremely convenient considering it gives you plenty of time to rush home and take the phone off the hook to avoid getting involved.

You are as dedicated a social climber as either Aries or Capricorn; however, you have neither Aries' honesty or Cappy's class. But since you haven't the faintest glimmer of self-awareness, you quite cheerfully assume that no one thinks your sudden interest in an eighty-five-year-old Lotto winner is odd.

Libra is the sign of the actor, double agent, transvestite, and paid escort. You also make excellent politicians because of your ability to talk out of both sides of your mouth at once.

You are a font of useless minutiae, forever analyzing your problems, like a cow chomping its cud. You treat the people you love like projects and take perverse pleasure in pointing out their faults, then get offended when they tell you to piss off. You play the If Only game. "You have such beautiful eyes. If only you'd lose some weight, we might be able to see them." "You are so kind-hearted. If only you had the common sense to match." And you are so shallow that your feelings get hurt if someone skips your party to check into the hospital for emergency surgery.

Since you inherited Venus' bed-hopping perspective on romance, you have secret affairs with people with whom you wouldn't be caught dead in public. That's OK with you because you're so vain that you rationalize one night with you will magically improve their miserable lot in life. You long for a meaningful relationship, but anything less than blind agreement from the one you love sends you to bed with the nearest stranger. You don't want a partner; you want a clone. Old Libra couples are easy to spot because of their matching hairdos.

However, you are also capable of pursuing a goal with a single-minded determination that borders on obsession. Your deeply held beliefs set you apart from the rest of the world. Once you learn to avoid the petty jealousies and soap-opera theatrics in which you frequently indulge, you soon learn that no sign alive can distract you from your dreams.

Your rational and fair-minded opinions quickly reduce the

emotionally subjective Water signs, Cancer, Pisces, and Scorpio, to babbling incoherency. Earth signs, Capricorn, Taurus, and Virgo, find themselves grabbing at thin air when trying to lay heavy-handed judgments on your determined shoulders. Aries may belch fire and spew brimstone; however, their infantile posturing is quickly exposed and sent to bed without supper. Leo and Sagittarius' endless self-aggrandizing bores you to tears, and your detached rationality reduces them to the same. You and fellow Air signs, Aquarius and Gemini, understand each other on a soul level and, therefore, rarely have serious confrontations.

Your philosophy is "Peaceful co-existence." You seek balance and harmony, and see no point in giving in to the ravages of time. You believe in living in the moment versus planning an uncertain future. Let the rest of the world make its demands and take its stands. Years from now when the control freaks you've left behind are gumming mashed potatoes at Sunny Acres, you will be in Switzerland getting your annual dose of sheep placenta and shushing down the Alps with your newest lover.

It's ALL Relative—The Libra Family

> It's very important to have the right clothing to exercise in. If
> you throw on an old T-shirt or sweats, it's not inspiring for your
> workout.
>
> CHERYL TIEGS (SEPTEMBER 27)

Living in a Libra household is the best exercise in frustration a kid can get. Libra parents are never satisfied. Your hair will be too long or too short. Your friends will never be good enough. And when you fall in love, don't expect their approval. These folks will complain that your doctor fiancée works too many hours or your teacher spouse doesn't make enough money.

They will be in a constant dither over whether they should keep you under lock and key until you are twenty-five or let you move into a commune as soon as you hit puberty. Mom will be obsessed with your appearance, because it's a reflection on her. Dad will either hover over your every movement or not remember you still live at home. Neither will give you the same answer twice, and both will meddle in your life until they are dead.

Even Libra toddlers have difficulty making decisions. If yours gets cranky when you are trying to teach him how to dress himself, it's because you've given him too many choices. Choose his outfit, tell him in what order to get dressed, and he will happily and quickly master the task. The same goes for toys, ice cream, and cartoons. As your Libra grows, help them make small decisions, and you will prepare them to make bigger ones as adults.

Your Libra teen will challenge every rule. The wisest thing that you can do is think carefully before making a rule, then stick to it. All Libras were born with a lawyer's instinct for finding a flaw in an argument, and puberty is the best time to teach yours that not everything is open for discussion. He or she will push you to the limit, but if you are fair in both your expectations and your punishment, you'll have little serious trouble.

Libra siblings hog the bathroom, spend hours in front of the mirror, and use your perfume or shaving lotion without asking. They talk on the phone all evening, fall in and out of love on a startlingly regular basis, and never make up their minds. You learned as a toddler that they argue over everything just for fun, so avoid eye contact and slip on your headphones whenever they appear.

Surviving a Libra home requires patience, diplomacy, and reason. And you are the person who must exhibit these traits, because none of your Libra relatives have them. You'll survive unscathed if you let the small stuff slide and plan ahead for the things you really want. Your Libra parents mean well even though they drive you bonkers with their indecisiveness. However, they will agree to disagree when you decide to go to college in the next state. Once you get there, you'll realize you're the best-dressed kid on campus.

Office Party—Bitches, Snitches, and the Chronically Inert

There is no human problem which could not be solved if people would simply do as I advise.

GORE VIDAL (OCTOBER 3)

Libra bosses pit the staff against one another to keep everyone off guard. He will poll the entire office before announcing a decision he has already chosen in order to have somewhere to lay blame if it turns out wrong. He or she will never give you a direct answer. Instead you'll get a vague, calculated, deliberately confusing response. Ask for clarification and you'll find yourself on the cold end of a smug lecture about the wisdom of taking notes.

Executive Libra will also dispense plenty of free advice about your personal life, the way you arrange your desk, and your choice of lunch companions. He or she will tell you how to dress, point out that you've gained a bit of weight lately, and not so discreetly let it slip that they disapprove of your taste in friends.

A Libra in charge will have the most expensive office furniture the company budget will allow. Everyone else will have pressboard desks and manual typewriters. Your Libra boss will consider himself as wise and diplomatic as Gandhi, but his smirking observations more closely resemble Groucho Marx. His best friend will be the manager in charge of expense accounts, and you'll rarely see him after lunch because he's dedicated himself to personally inspecting every pickup joint in town.

Your Libra coworker will be too busy gossiping on the phone, writing personal correspondence, or grabbing a quickie with the UPS deliveryman to think about grabbing your job. However, when you pick up the slack because she's stretched her lunch hour into half the afternoon, running her dog to the groomer and her grandmother to the hairdresser, she'll think you are after *her* job. In that case, she'll decide to get you fired. Right after she gets a manicure.

At the nail salon, she'll cool down and decide it's best if she just says thanks. When she returns and discovers the boss asked you to finish the annual report, she'll sneer and demand to meet with her supervisor because she feels threatened by your obvious attempts to get her canned. Just before she flits into his office, a business crisis will occur, and she'll decide it wouldn't be fair to him to complain about you right now. Since this scenario will continue as long as you have a Libra coworker, you really don't have much to worry about.

To irk this irritating, dithering bimbo, flip her office air-conditioning from one extreme to the other whenever you walk by. Do the same thing with the ringer on her phone and the volume on her radio. Say good morning one day and ignore her the next. When she's totally off balance, rush up to her desk and say, "The boss has two projects that need immediate attention. Pick one. Now."

Can't We All Get Along?

Short of entering therapy from sheer frustration, how can you tolerate living with a human seesaw? Easy, once you make up your mind.

Self-indulgent Libras

What others view as extravagance is really Libra's effort to create a space that satisfies their need for comfort and calm. Unfortunately, expensive furniture and lots of accessories soothe them best. When yours is considering a budget-busting purchase, instead of cutting up the credit cards, appeal to their sense of fair play.

First, point out that buying the four-thousand-dollar sofa he or she has been lusting after would mean eating peanut butter and jelly for the next twelve years. Next, offer a compromise, such as a less-expensive piece of furniture and a semi-expensive piece of artwork for the wall. Libras like to negotiate, so be prepared to spend the next several hours, or weeks, driving around town looking for all sorts of interesting stuff. And be aware, while you are trying to save money, Libra will be secretly hoping that a bit of his or her love of the luxurious rubs off.

Irresolute Libras

All Libras are born with a highly changeable nature. What made them laugh this morning will irk them this afternoon. What they adored last week, they despise today. They also spend a great deal of time trying to be all things to all people. This isn't only frustrating to you; it's just as confusing to them. Libras often suffer depression and feel isolated because they view their need to weigh the pros and cons as a weakness.

Think about their metaphorical symbol, the Scales. If you've seen real scales in action, you will know that they are never totally motionless unless totally out of whack. They dip first to one side, then the other. And, depending upon how much weight they are trying to balance, the dips become deeper and swing back slower.

Your Libra's emotional structure is identical. When they are weighted down with a serious issue, listen carefully as they explain the situation. Then offer a strong opinion without being threatening. This will give Libra the push he or she needs to see that side of the argument in a clearer light, then to re-examine the opposite side more rationally. They won't allow you to make their decisions for them, but by playing Devil's Advocate, you'll save them, and yourself, lots of time and grief.

Vain Libras

A Libra who hasn't learned that true beauty comes from within is not a pretty sight. And even the sweetest ones have a tendency to equate the superficial with substance. Libras crave admiration and attention. They never forget a compliment and thrive when they feel wanted and appreciated. At the same time, they may withhold those very things from others, dispense unfair criticism, and judge people by their appearance, job, or home, instead of taking time to get to know them.

Keep yours balanced with frequent praise and little surprises. Indulge their sense of romance by taking them out at least once a week. If they exhibit their petulant, jealous, and petty traits, remind them that part of the reason you admire them so much is their ability to judge impartially and treat every human with respect and equality.

Illogical Libras

Libras of both sexes and all ages have the exasperating trait of making a perfectly sound decision, then going off the deep end at the last minute and doing the exact opposite. For example, your Libra teen may save all year for a down payment on a car, then blow every penny on a weekend at the beach with his friends.

This action appears totally irresponsible and illogical. Actually, while your teen may not have thought long, he did consider the idea and understand the consequences. A flash of Libra intuition prompted him. He is young, the weather is perfect, the friends he holds dear have gathered, and on a level he can't explain he knows occasions such as this one are rare in life.

Quick Tips for Emergencies
- ♎ Libras need harmony.
- ♎ Good manners are the key to getting their attention.
- ♎ Frequent praise keeps them smiling.
- ♎ Never force them to make snap decisions.

☋ Gaslight them by telling them their horoscope doesn't agree with their fortune cookie.

Libra Lovers and Losers
Ma Barker
Dr. Joyce Brothers
Charlie Brown
Divine
Lynette "Squeaky" Fromme
Heinrich Himmler
Evel Knievel
Jerry Lee Lewis
Bela Lugosi
Lee Harvey Oswald

Chapter Nine

Scorpio

October 23–November 21

Let the Games Begin

Element: Water. Scorpio Water is a bottomless, roiling paradox. Fall in without protective armor and you'll come out a skeleton.

Quality: Fixed. Scorpios never forget, forgive, or let go.

Symbol: Scorpion. Just as its crusty little namesake, the human version will destroy itself trying to get revenge.

Ruler: Pluto and Mars. Suspicious hothead. Compulsive-obsessive two-timer.

Favorite Pastime: Plotting their next move.

Favorite Book: *The Klingon Guide to Mercy.*

Role Model: The Masked Avenger.

Dream Job: Judge, jury, and lord high executioner.

Key Phrase: "I'll get you for that."

Body Part: Sex organs. Terminal case of the seven-year itch. Scratches frequently.

Approach with Caution

Scorpio, the eighth sign of the zodiac, lives in the House of Death, Sex, and Other People's Possessions. Conventional astrology describes Scorpio as an intense, mysterious, sensual creature blessed with the gift of regeneration, like Phoenix rising from its ashes. Make that Dracula rising from the coffin. Rotten Scorpios are obsessed, stealthy, corporal control freaks who replenish their egos at everyone else's expense.

Scorpio has two ruling planets. Mars, the god of conflict and aggression, bestows a primed, suspicious character. That friendly surface is separated from a boiling miasma of emotion by only a couple of layers of very thin skin. Pluto, the god of extremes, instills an unmatched instinct for survival. Wooden stakes, holy water, or a stretch in the pen—nothing can harm Scorpio but Scorpio itself.

Scorpio's favorite game is Kangaroo Court. They subscribe to the Salem witch trial version of justice. Die and you're innocent. Live and you're guilty. Feel free to ignore yours as you would a petulant teenager. He or she will bite his or her own foot awhile, then curl up in the nearest dark corner and go to sleep.

Scorpios are extreme, not rational. They view life as either black or white and rarely compromise. Being born with the all-or-nothing gene has voided their ability to form lasting relationships with anyone who refuses to submit to their control. Argue with one, and suffer a verbal beating that makes you wish they had slugged you instead. Prove your point, and they will give themselves an ulcer trying to get even.

If You Love One—Scorpio Man

If only I had a little humility, I would be perfect.

TED TURNER (November 19)

Whether he is tall, dark, and handsome or short, blond, and chubby, a Scorpio man is idealistic, passionate, and loyal. He will mesmerize you with his candid, purposeful stare and capture your heart with his magnetic charm. He may be as cuddly as Sinbad, or as sexy as Leonardo DiCaprio; wear a white collar, a blue collar, or no collar at all; but here is the man who is impossible to resist. Think you've hit the jackpot? Think again, sweetheart. Loving a male Scorpion is like falling for King Kong.

Oh, he's sexy and, underneath that aloof exterior, surprisingly sensitive. Of course, that tidbit of knowledge may not help when you are handed divorce papers because you said his best friend was a low-life slob. Other guys might sit down to discuss their feelings. Mr. Intense will sit down and rip yours to shreds.

He is selfish. Never mind that you are married to him or in a serious relationship. The Scorpion's idea of commitment is showing up for dinner most of the time. His emotion switch is set at subzero and he won't hesitate to be unfaithful until he's dead. However, contrary to popular belief, he is not sex-crazed. That trait belongs to cousin Aries. Scorpio is terrified of deep emotional dependence on just one person, so, in his usual ass-backward way, he screws around precisely to avoid intimacy.

A male Scorpion has two reasons for living. The first is power. The second is control. He would control fate if he could—and some try. He will usually be a good provider because his desire for power and control drives him to become successful in his chosen profession. But money is rarely his primary motivation. Financial gain is only a by-product of becoming Mr. Big.

His moods change faster than a Pisces flipping the remote, and he will test your love by demanding the devotion of a religious fanatic at a revival meeting. He's so jealous, possessive, and sarcastic that you will be tempted to poison his oatmeal. There's no handling a Scorpion. You either put up with him or run like hell.

Deliberately awaken this man's green-eyed monster, and

you better have a shovel handy. You are going to need it to either defend yourself or dig your own grave. Remember this before you are foolish enough to plunge into an affair, or worse, a legally binding relationship.

The worst thing you can do to a Scorpio man is to not react to his emotional intimidation tactics. If he demands to be alone, applaud. Curb his sarcasm with a yawn. If he says he wants an open marriage, tell him you thought you already had one. When he announces he's going out without you, tell him to have a good time, then smile as if you know something he doesn't. He'll pretend to leave, park around the block, and sneak back to lurk in the bushes, convinced that you are cheating on him. He's as obtuse as Taurus when he thinks he's right and will stand in a rainstorm all night, muttering to himself, while you are cozy by the fireplace.

He communicates by threat. The foremost one is that he's leaving you. He also lies. The only thing harder to rid yourself of than a Scorpio man is a Cancer woman.

A male Scorpion frequently looks like he just ate a cactus. That's because he spends half his life getting even for some real, or imagined, slight and the other half causing all his own troubles.

Consider Scorpio Teddy Roosevelt. During a summer break from Harvard, eighteen-year-old Roosevelt entertained several friends from New York, including Edith Carow, a girl for whom he had great affection. Unfortunately, Edith (a Leo) flirted with several of his friends during the festivities, and Teddy reacted like a typical Scorpio. He married someone else. After his first wife died, again in classic Scorpio style, Teddy sought his first love. They were married for thirty-three years and had five children.

Yours will be so secretive that he would rather have his fingernails pulled out than tell you what he had for lunch. He's morbidly afraid that if he dares to share any serious facts, or fears, you may get the upper hand. That's why he's so good at small talk. He can blather for hours about every piece of minutiae in the world, but ask him a direct question, and he will clam up and rush outside to mow the lawn.

Your home will be either near water or hidden in a cul-de-sac behind a tall fence. He would live in a place that's accessible only by helicopter, except that it would screw up his Thursday-night dates with the cocktail waitress at the Bowl-O-Rama.

If you do catch him between the wrong pair of sheets, he will put on such a display of groveling, whining, and begging that you might think he's suffered a breakdown. Don't be fooled. He thrives on intensity and is as much masochist as manipulator. He will do anything it takes at that moment to gain your forgiveness, except change. Scorpio is Fixed Water. He exists in a bottomless well of churning emotional excess and is so embroiled in trying to figure out his own emotions that he will never understand yours.

Being sucked into the vortex of his charm is akin to getting lost in the Bermuda Triangle. You may or may not survive the trip.

If You Love One—Scorpio Woman

I'm tired of all these wussy guys, wringing their hands.
HILLARY RODHAM CLINTON (OCTOBER 26)

There is nothing superficial about a female Scorpio. She is a woman of total confidence and grace. Her style is all classic chic, her manner friendly but reserved. She expects you to be strong, courageous, and ambitious. She is psychically astute and can sense the subtlest of changes in your mood, and pinpoint the cause, with the skill of a trained psychoanalyst.

That's the good part. The rotten part is that Ms. Scorpio graduated from the Hannibal Lecter School of Therapy. She dispenses her opinions in a way that crushes your ego and destroys your pride in one fell swoop, much like chopping off your finger to cure a hangnail. She fears nothing, questions everything, and will go to the ends of the earth for a friend or lover. She could read the Bible to the Devil and make him listen.

All Scorpio women instinctively know that the fastest way to a man's heart is through his ribcage. Home may be your torture chamber, but it's her sanctuary. Don't ever betray this woman. Don't threaten her or in any way endanger her security. And for God's sake, don't publicly humiliate her. There are women scorned and then there are Scorpio women scorned, and a betrayed female Scorpion is like Lady Macbeth on crack.

Consider Betty Broderick's story, as researched by Joseph Geringer. Broderick told authorities, "I bought the program hook, line, and sinker—big sinker! Marry the man of your dreams . . . a good provider. I viewed everything as us. Dan never seemed to have that view. In the divorce, all the debts were fifty percent mine, but all the assets were one hundred percent his. I realize now that he was right when he said our battles would continue until one of us was gone." In case you don't remember, she is the lady who killed her lawyer ex-husband and his new, younger wife in 1989 after a particularly nasty, and public, divorce.

Your female Scorpion will mostly likely not reach for a gun, but she will make you reach for hard liquor in a tall glass.

She is so politically astute, she can instantly analyze a room full of your peers and tell you exactly who will help further your ambitions and whom to avoid. In fact, she will manipulate both you and your career so skillfully you'll think you ended up chairman of the board all by yourself. Not so. The female Scorpion craves power as much as her male counterpart and usually has a hidden agenda of her own. She will not hesitate to help you achieve your goals so she can achieve hers. Just ask Leo Bill Clinton.

She is also sullen, congenitally depressed, and has a penchant for staring into space for so long that you'll think she's catatonic. She is as cagey and manipulating as her sister Water signs, Pisces and Cancer. However, Ms. Scorpion will not hesitate to sleep her way to the top, if that's the only ride she can get. She lives for scandal and can often be found at public executions or reading trashy tabloids.

Romantically, her sexuality is sensual and her desire is to merge with a man who is her equal. Trouble is she never considers any man her equal. She will try to make you her doormat and, when you are face down in the mud, tap dance on your back in her red stilettos. With a Scorpio woman, the best way to keep your love new is to give her a fresh coat of varnish once a month and keep her out of direct sunlight.

If You Are One-Born Rotten

Never give up. And never, under any circumstances, face the facts.

Ruth Gordon (October 30)

Why is your life so difficult? Because you are still repaying the bad karma you earned the last go-around, when you were Torquemada's rack-master during the Inquisition.

Your exaggerated nature provides extremes of every kind. Compulsions and obsessions explode within your psyche. A startlingly large number of you either become geniuses, or sink into the lowest depths of depravity. You latter types make ideal mates for Pisces.

Your favorite TV shows are reruns of *Dark Shadows* and you wear a Barnabas Collins ring on your forefinger. You love to point randomly at unsuspecting strangers and mumble gibberish. Your moods range from irritable to pissed off, and you frequently sulk, brood, intimidate, spy, and cheat. That's on one of your good days. Unlike Taurus, who is blind to his faults, you are acutely aware of your flaws, but excessively proud of them. For instance, you like to wear a minipicture of your mug shot on a gold chain.

Being a Fixed sign means that your emotions and opinions rarely change. You are kindly described as "still water runs deep." You more closely resemble a boiling cesspool of hydrochloric acid. Your metaphorical stinger is always poised for attack and you are supposedly known for vicious verbal barbs. In reality, most of you are merely cantankerous bores who constantly posture and gouge lines in the dirt daring others to step across.

You are so private even your relatives don't know your unlisted phone number. You have a NO SOLICITORS sign on the barbed-wire fence around your property, and anyone attempting to reach your front door will need a map and a flashlight to make it through the overgrowth. You are so paranoid that you think Alcatraz would be a safe place to live.

Scorpios have bumper stickers that say things like, "My child sells drugs to your honor student." You are chronically terse, and have *Bad Ass, Son of Bad Ass,* or *Mother of Bad Ass* tattooed on your neck.

You keep a police scanner on the kitchen table to track the movements of your friends—both of them. Instead of family pictures, your refrigerator is covered with magnetic business cards of lawyers, therapists, and bail bondsmen. Inside is a mishmash of variety ranging from mashed potatoes to granola bars. Your eating habits swing as wildly as your emotions, from Spartan bark eater to comfort-food junkie.

Scorpio is the sign of the prosecuting attorney, psychopath, Mafia negotiator, and more-parts-than-you-were-prepared-to-lose surgeon. Scorpios also make good stalkers, astrologers, and psychics; however, very few of you are in the latter profession because you refuse to acknowledge your clairvoyance.

You follow Scorpio Adam Ant's views on sex. He said, "I like sex. My songs are about sex . . . sex is my life. I just find it the most exhilarating experience, and I think it should be done on stage." You'd join his band if you could.

You are the most intense of all signs. Telling you to learn to go with the flow, or to lighten up, is ridiculous. Control is your forte. Learn to use it on yourself before running over your children, friends, and lovers with your steel-belted emotions, and you'll quickly discover that most people like to be around you because of the sheer force of your personality.

When angered, you can slay every sign walking with alarming ease. Earth signs fall like dominos before you. Nervous Virgo won't survive one round of your not-so-subtle sarcasm. Capricorn and Taurus may try to intimate, or bellow, but wither under one of your intense tell-it-like-it-is sessions. You easily drive Air signs Gemini and Aquarius out of their minds with frustrated fury. And the first list of suggested improvements Libra hands you will find its way right up their pointy little nose. Your well-chosen sarcasms sting worse than any Lion's claw. You quash Sagittarius' armchair philosophizing with one or two brutal facts of life, and Aries' childish angst is no match for your verbal stinger. You and the other Water signs, Cancer and Pisces, understand each other on a soul level, and therefore, rarely have serious confrontations.

Your philosophy is "Mind your own business." You are guided by instinct and driven by passion. Let the rest of the world spend its time on frivolous pursuits and TV game shows; you are too busy quietly forging a solid gold future. Years from now when your ex-lovers and other strangers are playing shuffleboard, and remembering sex with a nostalgic sigh, you can send them pictures of yourself, one hand squeezing the bottom of your twenty-something sweetheart, the other accepting the award for Sexiest Senior Citizen in Rio.

It's All Relative–The Scorpio Family

Speak softly and carry a big stick.

THEODORE ROOSEVELT (OCTOBER 27)

Living in a Scorpio-ruled household is like being a permanent guest on the *Jerry Springer Show*. We'll discuss Aquarius Jerry's taste for the perverse a few chapters from now, but the essence of the show is pure Scorpionic Hell.

A nest of Scorpions contains at least one family member who is on drugs, in jail, or a guest of the psycho ward, as well as various afflicted friends and relatives who show up at all hours of the day and night or call for help from the last telephone booth in the Mojave Desert.

Scorpio parents pride themselves on telling The Truth. They may insist that you get a job raking lawns so you can pay room and board. The fact that you are five years old is of little consequence. Scorpio parents believe that it's never too early for The Truth. They, on the other hand, will be too busy spending money on the latest race car or ski boat to sock away any for your college tuition. To avoid the repo-man, or the last guy your father beat the hell out of, you'll move frequently.

Scorpio Roseanne Barr is supposed to have said, "I have five kids from three different marriages. I come from a trailer park; my sister and brother are both gay; I have multiple personalities; and the *National Enquirer* reunited me with my daughter, who I had given up for adoption." Sounds like a typical Pluto/Mars–ruled family to me.

Dad loves you, but can't relate beyond alternately criticizing and yelling. He's a stern father, but will also be there for you right or wrong. In another of the Scorpion's dubious virtues, Dad will defend you even if you are a car thief or a drug dealer, but will never think to steer you toward either a classroom or professional help.

Mom will alternate between lecturing you into a coma and rationalizing your bad behavior with a hundred varied excuses. Yet both parents will be genuinely surprised if you drop out of high school in favor of pumping gas or joining the Mafia.

As all Water-sign parents, Scorpios see every fault of every human except those they love. Mark Twain said, "Denial ain't just a river in Egypt." He may have been a Sagittarius, but this quote totally encompasses the Scorpion attitude toward family.

A Scorpion baby is silent and observant. Don't mistake quiet for acquiescing. Your little Scorpio is sizing up the odds, and absorbing all the family dynamics even before he or she can talk. By that time, if you haven't as yet established who is boss, you will soon find out.

A Scorpio teen will try to control the household, either by subtle emotional manipulation or out and out juvenile delinquent behavior. And once out of control, you might as well relax and forget it. This kid has his or her own agenda and you won't be able to figure it out, much less change it. The best thing to do is the day they are born start molding your child's personality in favor of the good side of the force. Better yet, talk to her while she is still in the womb.

Your Scorpio siblings will be so moody you won't know what, or who, to expect when you walk in the door. One day your brother or sister may be your pal and help clean your room. The next he, or she, may snip off a piece of your hair to affix to a voodoo doll that's scarily in your likeness.

Hey, look on the bright side. After you've survived a Scorpio-ruled household, anything else you encounter for the rest of your life will seem like a piece of cake.

Office Party–Bitches, Snitches, and the Chronically Inert

I have no responsibility to be politically correct.
Demi Moore (November 11)

Working for a Scorpio is like working for the Mafia. He or she will usually have a reserved demeanor, be as soft-spoken as the Godfather, and expect the same kind of unwavering loyalty. Both are shrewd, driven, and hardworking. Both want power more than money and control more than public recognition. Just like his mob counterpart, on the surface, Boss Scorpion is congenial, hospitable, and well dressed. He also invented the phrase *Hostile Takeover.*

A Scorpio boss is not the delegating type. She will toss a project on your desk, but will also control every step of its production. Your job is to defer to her judgment, say, "Yes, master," frequently, and keep the coffee pot on high all night.

You may never know where, or if, this boss went to college, is married, divorced, gay, or straight. However, you will find yourself spilling your guts about your latest romance, the dog, the landlord, and your past life as a go-go-dancer under the mesmerizing stare and subtle questioning of the Scorpion-in-charge.

Having a Scorpio coworker is like being in the cold war with a double agent. The only person she's loyal to is herself. She may be your best friend, lunch companion, or faithful assistant, but if she decides that the next place up the corporate ladder she should occupy is the rung you're sitting on, you will rarely guess, until it's nearly, or actually, too late to save yourself. He or she is prepared to wait, plot, and plan every move.

The best thing for you to do is be friendly but wary of every Scorpio coworker. Even the one whom you think is your best friend. Especially if he or she begins to ask subtle questions like what kind of wine the boss drinks.

Irking a Scorpio is easy. Treat them like they treat everyone else. Be aloof, remote, and act superior. Stare at them a lot. Once they realize they can't intimidate you, they will entertain themselves by shooting rubber bands at the mailroom clerk.

Can't We All Get Along?

With Scorpio, you have to be willing to take the whole package. You aren't going to change them, but you can survive quite nicely if you learn to play the game.

Vengeance-Is-Mine Scorpions

As do all Water signs, Scorpio overreacts first, then may, or may not, think later. But, a Scorpion's primary impulse is to verbally, or physically, attack, then sever the relationship, whether it's personal, professional, or the guy next door who innocently commented that those black roses looked a bit harsh in the garden.

This is because all Scorpios are born with a morbid fear of rejection. This knowledge, however deeply buried within your Scorpion's psyche, is the primary motivating force behind their actions. They operate from the get-them-before-they-get-you perspective. To complicate matters, as a Fixed sign, their beliefs and opinions rarely change.

Repeatedly remind yours that a difference of opinion is not synonymous with trying to humiliate, rebuff, or challenge him or her. This takes courage and patience. Sooner or later yours will learn the difference between harmless dissent and pointed opposition. They may still wince at an opposing view-point, but they will have learned to agree to disagree.

Control-Freak Scorpions

Scorpios' complex emotional structures make them so afraid of losing control of their internal feelings that they must micro-manage every external event. Scorpios are acutely aware of, and frequently horrified by, their own vulnerability, which they view as some sort of character flaw. They may act impervious to an emotional crisis, which seems like an act of cruel and selfish behavior, but is actually a total act of self-preservation.

Sounds sappy, after all that tough-guy or -gal posturing. But next time yours is grumping about the way the dishwasher is loaded, or staring, stiff lipped out the window because the dog had to stay overnight at the vet's, take them by the hand. You don't have to say anything, and they may or may not speak, either. But they won't let go and next time their feelings are hurt, they will be more likely to tell you what's wrong and less likely to pick a fight over the laundry bill.

Sexy Scorpions

Legend says that Scorpios are voracious sexual predators who would rather score than eat, sleep, or breathe. Fact is that the percentage of Scorpios who compulsively cheat is probably no more than any other sign; it's just that when they are bad, they tend to be very bad. However, they are sensual, sexual creatures and if they don't feel loved at home, even the best-intentioned ones are capable of occasionally straying.

Keeping yours interested is easy. Every Scorpio alive is surprisingly susceptible to flattery. They act aloof, but secretly crave attention. Tell yours he or she is wonderful, smart, and gorgeous. Surprise with a whimsical gift. Keep the lights on low, jazz on the sound system, and the phone unplugged. Slip on a little nothing in black, gray, or maroon; splash on a scent with a dangerous name; and you'll have Mr. or Ms. Scorpio's undivided attention tonight, tomorrow, and for as long as you want it.

Hermit Scorpions

Scorpios are the most private sign in the zodiac. They crave a stable and safe home, where they can let down their guard, relax, and feel protected. They hate unexpected company, including relatives and/or friends who drop by unannounced. Also, Scorpions are basically loners who may occasionally isolate themselves from you, too. This can manifest as anything from sitting in the backyard all evening staring at the stars to expressing a desire for separate vacations.

Understanding that their motives are usually honest can help you wave good-bye when they head for the beach alone. Helping them understand that two can share solitude as peacefully as one will help them discover how nice being alone with you can be.

Quick Tips for Emergencies

♏ Scorpions need unconditional love.

♏ Patience is key to winning their confidence.

♏ Calm them by listening without judging.

♏ Flattery will get you everywhere.

♏ Gaslight them by mirroring their actions and/or ignoring them.

Serious And Serious-About-Sex Scorpions

Pat Buchanan

Larry Flynt

John Gotti

Tonya Harding

Shere Hite

Charles Manson

George S. Patton

RuPaul

Bram Stoker

Ike Turner

Chapter Ten

Sagittarius

November 22–December 21

More Than You Ever Wanted to Know About Anything

Element: Fire. Sagittarius Fire is a bank of glowing embers. Its smoldering warmth appears comforting, but try to cozy up to it, and you'll soon be dodging a barrage of sparks.

Quality: Mutable. Has a swinging-door attitude toward life— the bedroom door.

Symbol: The Archer. Sagittarius is the hunter of the zodiac. Bargain hunter, sexual predator.

Ruler: Jupiter. Larger-than-life. Brutally frank. Chronically gauche.

Favorite Pastime: Opening mouth before engaging brain.

Favorite Book: *The One-Minute Philosopher.*

Role Model: Urkel.

Dream Job: Senator in charge of filibusters.

Key Phrase: "Did I do that?"

Body Part: Lower back, chronically aching from being such a pain in the ass.

Approach with Caution

Sagittarius lives in the Ninth House of Philosophy, Adventure, and Long-Distance Travel. In astrological myth, this Mutable Fire sign is described as a gregarious, honest fun-lover who was born with a philosophical outlook and a yen to wander. The rotten truth is this tactless, vociferous bore galumphs through the world with one foot caught in a bucket and the other lodged firmly between his, or her, overdeveloped jaws.

Jupiter, supreme god of the Universe, rules Sagittarius, and here this over-the-top jolly joker bestows a restless nature and extravagant personality. Both sexes think they know everything and spend their time trying to educate the rest of us.

They don't do subtle. Archers have outrageous horse laughs, louder than the din of Times Square on New Year's Eve, and a court-jester smile. Prod beneath that slapstick grin and you'll release a ton of repressed fury. All of that suppressed rage is why Sagittarius makes the world's best serial killer. Like one of Jupiter's thunderbolts, an Archer's anger is both unpredictable and finished as soon as it cracks through the air to deafen you. Luckily, your average Sadge blows his, or her, top infrequently and, instead of physical violence, prefers to put a fist through the door and shout vile epithets about your family heritage.

Archers are passionate, not stable. By chasing whatever attracts them at the moment, they often fall victim to their own penchant for vicarious thrills. Being born with the greener-pastures gene has skewed their perspective of long-term stability versus short-term sensation. Argue, and you'll suffer a lecture that will make your ears bleed. Try to prove your point, and you'll be left talking to yourself because your Centaur will have already jumped the nearest fence in search of fresh clover.

If You Love One—Sagittarius Man

My divorce came as a complete surprise to me. That will happen when you haven't been home in eighteen years.

LEE TREVINO (DECEMBER 1)

He's honest, trusting, and eternally optimistic. He won't restrict your freedom, or expect you to drop your nights out with friends in favor of staying home with him. He may have a wry perspective on life similar to Mark Twain's or the diplomacy of Winston Churchill. An Archer wants a companion to accompany him on frequent, spontaneous outings to wonderfully diverse places, because to him, life is to be explored and enjoyed.

Before you decide he's your soul mate, understand that a male Sagittarius has the same attitude toward commitment as does his mythological symbol, the Centaur. He spends all of his youth and most of his adulthood in continual heat. He is an accomplished lover, but it's the deed he desires, not you.

You no doubt fell for his Boy Scout smile and talent for quoting Shakespeare while simultaneously unfastening your bra. But, as a partner, he makes a great friend, one you won't see very often because his idea of home is a place to drop in when he needs a change of clothes or a shower. Since an Archer could happily live in a cave for months, eating crickets and contemplating his navel, even if you marry him, you'll feel like you're still single.

Don't expect to lean on his shoulder or cling to his arm. Do expect to be his pal (or groupie) and to spend many nights alone. He's neither jealous nor possessive. In fact, he wants you to have a life independent of his since that allows him more time for drinking beer with his buddies and following his favorite football team around the nation. He is the one guy in the Universe who was born to be a bachelor. He won't care how you dress, who your friends are, or where you spend your time, as long as you don't bother him with the details. He's too busy elucidating his latest theory for solving all the problems of the world.

Archers have opinions on every subject under the sun, and cannot answer even simple questions with a plain yes or no. Ask if he wants a ham sandwich, and he'll answer with the history of Earl of Sandwich, the sixteen different kinds of bread you could use to enhance the flavor of the meat, and a dissertation on mustard.

Michael de Nostradamus, the sixteenth-century French physician and mystic, had the distinct Sagittarian penchant for expounding on the mysteries of the Universe. In typical Archer style, the good doctor's visions were not only voluminous, totaling more than one thousand, but were carefully crafted, allowing endless interpretations. This ensured that whatever happened, he could be credited with prophesizing the event. Only an Archer would be as audacious and irresponsible as to predict events two thousand years into the future. And only an Archer could do it with such a flair for the art of bullshit.

A male Sagittarius respects authority, as long as he's the authority figure. Question his right to rule and you'll soon understand the meaning of Jupiter's wrath. He has a nasty temper and his volcanic eruptions result in expensive trips to the nearest home improvement center for wallboard, nails, and plaster.

He's impulsive. Send him out for milk, and he'll come home with reservations for the midnight flight to Peru. He might invite you along, and then again, he might tell you that since you both know he has more fun alone, he bought only one ticket. If he does take you, you will spend half your time dragging him out of the local hotspots where he's trading pickup lines with the natives and the other half tracking him through the jungle as he searches for the meaning of life. You'll be better off staying home hoping he gets kidnapped by pygmies.

The Archer's favorite game is Bad to Worse. Tell him the sink backed up, and he'll flood the basement because he forgot to turn off the water before he tore out the plumbing. Ask him to forgo one of his several nights out with the boys in favor of a quiet dinner at home, and he'll rant and rave that you are smothering his need for freedom.

Even lovable Archer Walt Disney had a dark side. Remember all those endearing fairy tales he brought to the screen? Bambi's dead mother and a raging forest fire. The orphaned Lion King stalked by his own family members. Snow White and Cinderella: One with a stepmother who wanted to cut her heart out, and the other who was forced to become a servant in her own home.

Yours will step on your toes, bore you with rhetoric, and hurt your feelings with a thoughtless remark. After all, he is a fire-breathing dragon. But, this guy is more like Pete's Dragon, Disney's character who flops along meaning no harm and leaving little lasting damage.

If You Love One—Sagittarius Woman

"How can you talk if you haven't got a brain?" asked Dorothy.
"I don't know. But some people without brains do an awful lot of talking, don't they?" answered the Scarecrow.

THE WIZARD OF OZ

She's the original Pollyanna. The Sagittarius woman is independent, optimistic, and believes that honesty is the best policy. She's not into self-pity, and you will find her genuine friendliness refreshing. She seeks a well-read, well-traveled partner. Picture a happy home, filled with laughter, spontaneity, and a woman who will accompany you to the ends of the earth.

Before you beg this bright little star to shine her light on you exclusively, please understand that not only is she afflicted with the same hoof-in-mouth disease as her male counterpart, all Sagittarian females are subject to a Twilight Zone–sort of serendipity that frequently causes them to be in the wrong place at the right time. She may not appear at dinner because she saw a cat stuck up a tree, dialed 911, and is trying to talk the firemen into letting her go up the ladder to rescue it.

She's also chronically late. If she gets up three hours early to be at your side before surgery, she'll get sidetracked into sorting the last six years' worth of phone bills into chronological order. Or, if she manages to make it out the door on time, she will have forgotten that today is also the neighborhood Cause-of-the-Month jog-a-thon, then forget you as she falls in step with her friends. She also falls down a lot, so don't be surprised if she's hobbling on crutches when she finally arrives at your bedside.

Her anger is like a flash fire that singes your eyebrows before you can drop and roll. Push her volcano button, and you will find yourself dodging assorted flying objects and buying a new set of glassware in the morning. She cools down rapidly but doesn't forget easily, and will most likely spend the next several months entertaining friends and family with a detailed account of the fight. Although she will have everyone howling with laughter, you will have learned that public humiliation is her way of punishing you for being such a jerk.

U.S. temperance advocate Carry Nation exemplifies both sides of the female Jupiter-ruled nature. During her pre-hatchet-wielding days she was known as Mother Nation, because of her generosity. One of her colleagues said, "Whatever she believes in she believes with her whole soul, and nothing except a superior force can stay her." When she joined the temperance movement, her typical Sagittarian lack of forethought and self-righteous arrogance surfaced. Her Jupitarian wrath was so formidable that boxing champion Libra John L. Sullivan hid from her when she marched into his upscale bar in New York City. Nation's bombastic wrath, independent personality, and unorthodox tactics were totally Sagittarian.

A female Archer can talk twenty minutes without stopping for air. She smiles so much you will think she's had plastic surgery from the same quack that stitched up the Joker. And she overloads her life with projects, parties, causes, and casual friendships because she can't stand to be alone.

She detests housework and most of the time your home will resemble the aftermath of a Level V tornado. Investing in a housekeeping service will keep the mold under control in the bathroom and ensure that you don't lose the children in the rubble.

In love, your lady Centaur likes affection but hates it if you try to smother her. She cherishes her freedom as much as the male, but is less apt to have either a wandering eye or body. However, she will have many assorted male friends whom she continues to phone and have lunch and share a movie with now and then. So, if you are a suspicious Scorpio, possessive Taurus, or arrogant Leo, you should think several times before considering this lady as a long-term mate because she will expect your trust and refuse to change her lifestyle. She is extremely passionate, but prefers sexual adventure to cloying emotional scenes.

Whether she's as outspoken as Jane Fonda or as outrageous as Bette Midler at her high-camp best, your lady Archer is the most independent female under the Sun.

If You Are One–Born Rotten

Get your facts first, and then you can distort them as much as you please.

MARK TWAIN (November 30)

You aren't happy unless you have a cause. Whether wiping out world hunger or fighting for more coconut doughnuts in the office snack box is immaterial, as long as you can unleash the force of Jupiter's self-righteous zeal.

You are the most capricious sign in the Universe. The fact that your frequent midnight treks for pizza and beer clad in nothing but your underwear has earned you your own code number with the local cops only enriches the list of outrageous stories you love to endlessly repeat to whimpering friends and family.

You don't do stable. Your threshold of boredom is so low that if anything in your life remains the same for longer than five minutes, you hyperventilate and head for the nearest exit. Your definition of *comfort zone* is the rest of the world's idea of *maniac mode*. Although you are basically a loner who loathes routine of any kind, you abhor solitude. This is because your Jupiter-ruled nature needs someone to look down on and order around. When forced to be alone, you subscribe to Sagittarius Frank Sinatra's philosophy of "I'm for anything that gets you through the night, be it prayer, tranquilizers or a bottle of Jack Daniel's."

Everything about you is exaggerated. *Honesty* means saying things such as "For a fat person, you sure don't sweat much." And your sense of adventure is limited to navigating the basement stairs without turning on the light. You talk about travel much more than actually going anywhere.

You are also the clumsiest sign alive. More accident-prone than an Aries in a sports car, your perpetually bruised head and scabby knees occur simply because you never pay attention. You stumble through life like Archer Emmett Kelly's sappy alter ego, breaking flowerpots with your head and dropping the good china on your bare feet trying to help do the dishes. But that's OK with you since you would rather be crippled for life than do anything the easy way.

You view romance as a race of how many, how fast. When you aren't flirting shamelessly with a married friend, you are getting engaged to three unlucky lovers simultaneously while making wedding plans with a fourth. And you are capable of leaving them all standing in the rain at the train station while you elope with the Leo in the gold jumpsuit you just met at the liquor store.

Sagittarius is the sign of the philosophy professor, travel agent, gypsy cab driver, and court jester. Archers also make excellent vagrants, snake oil salesmen, and joke writers for the Internet. Your ideal vacation spot is anywhere you don't have to bathe, shave, or cut your toenails.

You are also the optimist of the Universe who never loses sight of the end of the rainbow. You are positive, energetic, and full of good intentions. You need to learn to curb your proclivity to speak before you think, and fine-tune your excellent diplomatic skills. Once you understand the difference between trusting your luck and pushing your luck, nothing on earth can stop you. In battle, your aim is straight and your arrows are swift.

No Water sign alive can survive one of your off-the-cuff darts of honesty about their penchant for soppy sentimentalism. Cancer and Pisces visibly melt into the furniture. Scorpio's vitriolic stings can't penetrate your tough, Centaur hide. Earthy plodder Taurus sulks at your biting observation of their intolerant nature, and you leave critical Virgo and oppressive Capricorn in the dust when they try to corral your unbridled zest for adventure. One thrust of your flaming arrow of truth curbs Air signs Gemini and Libra's enthusiasm for verbal jousting. Cold-natured Aquarius is reduced to dissipating steam when it tries to freeze-dry your happy spontaneity. You and the other Fire signs, Aries and Leo, understand each other on a soul level and, therefore, rarely have serious confrontations.

Yours is the philosophy of, "He who laughs last laughs best." You believe in forgive-and-forget and rarely take life too seriously or for granted. Let everyone else grit their teeth, brawl, and battle. You are too busy forging toward your private dream and enjoying the journey to boot. Years from now when your enemies are in the nursing home, nursing their ulcers, you'll be dispensing your wisdom through a series of lectures on the *Love Boat,* and laughing—all the way to the bank.

It's ALL Relative—The Sagittarius Family

Adults are only kids grown up.

WALT DISNEY (DECEMBER 5)

It's not easy living in the house of brutal honesty. Your Sagittarius parents' tendency to expand every issue into gargantuan proportions, and habitual hour-long lectures over issues as inane as forgetting to take out the garbage can keep you too busy to get your homework done.

One light in this tunnel of verbosity is that Archer parents will start leaving you home alone as soon as you understand not to use the stove while they are gone. They feel they owe it to themselves because they stuck it out until you could work the remote control, and you'll be grateful for the silence while they're out scouring the swap meet for African death masks.

Mom will try to bribe you into staying honest and making good grades. Play her right and you could be driving a new car by the time you are a senior. Dad's favorite pastime is laying down the law on his way out the door for his yearly trek to hunt Big Foot in the high Sierra. Both continually spout ultimatums on which they never follow through.

There's no need to keep the lights dimmed or the room quiet for a Sagittarius baby. These toddlers sleep through the Super Bowl and awaken when the house is too quiet. Keeping a radio in their room helps them, and you, sleep through the night. Keep them safe with a helmet, kneepads, and elbow protectors, for they are extremely curious and too busy investigating everything within reach to exercise caution.

Be prepared for your Archer teen to cut the apron strings at an unusually early age. These kids were born to roam and to learn about life from living versus studying. The day after graduation yours may announce that he or she has joined the service or been accepted to a foreign university and that the plane leaves at midnight. And don't be surprised if he or she chooses the religious life. Jupiter-ruled children are the truth seekers of the Universe.

Sagittarius siblings spend their allowance on Monday and try to borrow yours on Tuesday. Don't fall for any promises of repayment or chore exchange to work off the debt. They mean well but are so scatterbrained they forget their promise as soon as the words leave their mouths. They are, however, good at helping you with your homework, and your anger at their chronic lack of tact and forethought will seldom last long. They learned as toddlers exactly what to say or do to make you grab your sides in laughter.

Survival in this home is easy. Encourage your parents to take many, many of those well-deserved trips and leave you in charge. Send your brother or sister to the movies with the allowance you traded them for doing your homework assignment. Then sit back, relax, and enjoy the quiet. Or call up a few friends and have a party. Either way, you've got it made.

Office Party—Bitches, Snitches, and the Chronically Inert

To succeed in life, you need two things: ignorance and confidence.

Mark Twain (November 30)

If life in a Sagittarius-ruled office were a movie, its title would be *The Keystone Cops Meet Frasier Crane.* Just like Frasier, Boss Archer is tactless, insensitive, and more interested in talking about himself than in listening to anyone else. Sagittarius bosses also habitually bite off more than they can chew, because they are too arrogant to admit they are overloaded and too tight to hire more help. This means you will continually operate at crisis speed.

He will wear a three-piece suit one day and spend his time in back-to-back meetings, then bring a sack with his fishing gear the next and tell you to clear his calendar so he can sneak off at noon. Since he believes in always telling the truth, he'll leave it to you to lie to his boss about why he's not at the weekly planning session.

Or she will spend all morning recounting the painful details of yesterday's appearance in divorce court, then come back from lunch and announce that she's engaged to her attorney.

Both will be genuinely surprised and appalled at how quickly work piles up on their desks, credenzas, and the floor. You, on the other hand, will have the Herculean task of trying to pin down these clowns long enough to get to the bottom of their In basket.

Archers are also the most easily distracted bosses in the Universe. They will drop anything for a chance to talk, and the subject doesn't matter. So if it's three o'clock and you are tired of pounding the keyboard, grab your coffee, close the door behind you, sit down, and say, "I'm listening."

Sagittarian coworkers are reckless, undependable, and hard to find, especially if there's a poker game going on in the maintenance room. They will talk on the phone all day, then ask for help to finish the project that's been in their In basket for a week.

Even though Sagittarius is a Fire sign, he or she is more backslapper than back-stabber. They view any job, even president of the company, as little more than a means of funding their next trip to the Andes. It's rare that one would try to usurp your position. But, if that were the case, he or she would probably blurt it out one afternoon. Then you'd say, "So, what's your plan?"

Irk one by refusing to listen to their constant chatter. Insist on total quiet, hand them your pile of reports to type if they stay on the phone more than five minutes, and turn off the overhead speakers so they can't hear the music. The next sound you hear will be their feet beating a path out the door.

Can't We All Get Along?

How do you exist under the same roof with a person who seems more suited to performing in the center ring of Barnum and Bailey than sitting next to you on the sofa? Once you know how to capture their attention, it's as easy as rolling off a log.

Talking-Head Archers

The caricature is a nonstop, nonthinking, blathering, jolly joker. The person is a friendly, cheerful, happy-hearted character. Sagittarians are the most outgoing of all signs because they genuinely like people. Even when they go overboard in the chatterbox department, they are nearly impossible to resist.

Help yours learn to listen, or at least take turns talking, by appealing to their sense of fair play. They are eager to please and will try hard to change, but if yours is an older model, you might want to keep the kitchen timer handy.

Free-Roaming Archers

Sagittarians absolutely despise being tied down, restricted, cooped up, or confined in any manner. The quickest way to start an argument is to tell yours that he or she can't go wherever it is he or she wants to go. Their need to physically escape, either for a short day trip or a weekend away, is part of their basic nature.

Though adventurers, Centaurs are not loners. Your Archer loves companionship and will be thrilled if you want to go along. Keep a backpack, filled with bottled water and nutritious snacks, handy for those all-day treks to the lake or antique fair—and an overnight bag of essentials in the closet that you can grab as you are being rushed out the door so you and your Archer can make it to the beach before the moon rises.

Playful Archers

Everything about a Jupiter-ruled character is expansive, including that charming personality. At parties they will circulate through the room laughing, twinkling, and shamelessly flirting. At lunch, all eyes will be on them as they happily amuse their friends. They are natural entertainers who have a keen wit and enjoy making others laugh. Being committed to you isn't going to make them change.

Suspect their motives, or worse, accuse them outright of being unfaithful, and you'll hurt them deeply. Understanding that the vast majority of Sagittarians operate from a personal honor system that puts the rest of the zodiac to shame should ease any doubts.

Should your jealous switch get stuck on high, tell your Archer how you feel. It won't stop the flirting. But to prove they love you, they will keep you in tow as they wander around the room at the next party. It may be a peculiar solution, but then everything about a Sagittarius is a bit off-the-wall.

Tact-Challenged Archers

Honesty is one of a Sagittarian's strongest virtues. Good judgment is a different story. No matter how ill chosen an Archer's remarks may be, there's usually not a shred of malice in his or her soul. This won't help much if you've just received one of those famous left-handed compliments. But knowing that this is truly a blind spot in their character might keep you from throwing the iron at his head.

Help yours be more aware by calling attention to their verbal faux pas each time one occurs. This will be easy, because one occurs about every ten minutes. Since Archers are very quick on the uptake, and hate to hurt anyone's feelings, with some patience on your part and minor effort on theirs, you can stretch that timeframe to about an hour.

Quick Tips for Emergencies

- ↗ Archers need adventure.
- ↗ Spontaneity is key to winning their hearts.
- ↗ Keep an overnight bag packed for spur-of-the-moment trips.
- ↗ Be a good listener.
- ↗ Gaslight them by insisting on total quiet.

Sagittarian Klowns and Killers

Billy the Kid
Ted Bundy
Crazy Horse
Howdy Doody (Buffalo Bob Smith)
Boris Karloff
Lucky Luciano
Harpo Marx
Mary, Queen of Scots
Babyface Nelson
Linda Tripp

Chapter Eleven

Capricorn

December 22–January 19

A Goat by Any Other Name

Element: Earth. Capricorn Earth is a mountain landscape filled with teetering boulders, deep crevices, and jutting rocks that the Goat nimbly maneuvers in a steady ascent. You, on the other hand, will get caught in a murderous landslide if you aren't strong enough to keep up.

Quality: Cardinal. Capricorn is headcheese.

Symbol: The Sea-Goat—half goat, half fish. Get your goat. Old goat. Wet blanket.

Ruler: Saturn, the god of hard knocks and cold, hard cash.

Favorite Pastime: Acting superior.

Favorite Book: *The Ten Secrets of World Dominion.*

Role Model: Mr. Freeze.

Dream Job: Scrooge's financial advisor.

Key Phrase: "One can never be too rich or too thin."

Body Part: Knees, permanently chaffed from kneeling at the mattress bank.

Approach with Caution

The House of Career and Public Recognition is home to the tenth sign of the zodiac, Capricorn. Generous astrological descriptions of the Sea-Goat include a conventional, determined, and purposeful person with a discriminating sense of taste and style. What you get is a pompous, domineering social climber, waving *Robert's Rules of Order* in one hand and a prenuptial agreement in the other.

Saturn rules Capricorn, and here, this ancient curmudgeon bestows a dogmatic, no-nonsense personality. Goats don't have lives; they have careers. These creatures are born with the same monomaniacal drive as the Goat half of their symbol, to be King of the Mountain. The Fishtail half signifies their "wet" emotional nature. This isn't soppy sentiment like a Water sign. It's a wet-blanket tendency to smother any feelings that surface. Goats regard emotionalism like slugs regard salt.

What they love is to recite the tale of how they pulled themselves up by their bootstraps to whatever position they currently hold. Of course, the fact that they were in the gutter and are now flipping hamburgers at the bus station is of no consequence. The pinnacle of a Goat's success is totally subjective.

Capricorn is serious, not spontaneous. By ignoring their need for emotional satisfaction, Goats often lose sight of life's intangible wealth in favor of its material goods. Being born with the is-that-all-there-is gene frustrates and depresses them, because after success comes the realization that life is meaningless without joy. Argue if you dare. Capricorns don't like to lose and will keep coming back for more until they triumph, or you throw up your hands in surrender. Prove one wrong . . . and expect a midnight phone call stating another counterpoint.

If You Love One—Capricorn Man

I'm a workaholic, and when I'm not working, I'm hiding in my basement.

HOWARD STERN (JANUARY 12)

He's strong, dependable, and a bit shy. Whether he's rich or poor, he dresses impeccably, acts like a gentleman, and most likely owns his own business. A male Capricorn will impress you with his reserved good manners. He may remind you of one of those old-time tough guys with a heart of gold, like Humphrey Bogart, and his favorite movie will probably be *It's a Wonderful Life*. Before you tear up over this sentimental fact, understand that the movie's evil banker, Mr. Potter, is the hero he's modeled his life after. Living with a Capricorn man is like being tied to a horsehair-upholstered armchair and forced to listen to a continuous loop of *Night on Bald Mountain*.

By the third date, he'll have decided whether or not he wants to make it permanent, which will have nothing to do with whether or not you feel the same way. Once he's fixed his beady little stare on you, he can make the most devoted Taurus look fickle.

Cappy loves applause as much as cousin Leo. However, where the Lion seeks adoration, the Goat sees it as an affirmation. No matter what means he uses to get where he's going, once he's there, he'll act like he's just one of the good old boys.

During Prohibition, Al Capone's bloodied climb to the top as King of the Bootleggers was unmatched in the annals of American crime. Capone dispatched friends and enemies alike with the same cold indifference. He was a model of Capricorn ruthlessness. But he also exhibited the Goat's need to be socially acceptable. He dressed more like a captain of industry than killer, and saw to it that his intimate circle of henchmen did likewise. Capone attended the opera, immersed himself in Chicago society, and tried his best to give the appearance of a benevolent bad boy just taking advantage of the times by supplying the relatively harmless vice of illegal liquor to an adoring public. In typical arrogant Capricorn style, Capone not only broke the law; he publicly dared the law to catch him. And though it finally did, Scarface Al didn't go to jail for bootlegging. He rode up the river on a tax-evasion charge, and history has it that once he was in Alcatraz, he became Boss Con.

Romantically, your Goat's basic attitude is that you should keep your mouth shut and your legs spread. Early in the relationship, he may forget himself and choke out an "I love you." Even if he marries you, he probably won't say it again. He will figure that if he made it legal and allowed you to quit your job so you could stay home to wait on him, that's proof enough.

Depending on his financial status, he'll have either a mini-office or a hotline to his bookie in the bedroom and will regulate your lovemaking with the same cool know-how he uses either in the boardroom or poolroom. He can be surprisingly passionate, once he feels comfortable enough to lose his inhibitions. But since he's not into role playing, sensual massage, or the use of mood-altering substances, you'll need the patience of a saint, and the persistence of a Virgo. It may take months to get him to lose the pajamas and quit shaking hands before jumping between the sheets.

He invented the double standard. The public credo of the FBI's head Goat, J. Edgar Hoover, was a bug in every bedroom and a rule for every action. The fact that Hoover publicly scorned any behavior that was a hairsbreadth left of fascism, and wore a dress in private, is a classic example of the Capricorn's code of conduct. It applies to everyone but himself.

He's condescending and totally oblivious to anyone's feelings but his own. He sees himself as the Great Patron and expects to control your checkbook, social calendar, and household schedule. He's so tight, he'll inspect the toothpaste tubes before you toss them away and make a once-a-week trip to the recycling center instead of using the curbside container.

Unless he's a chef or an auto mechanic, he won't shop for dinner or get his hands dirty changing the oil on the car. But he will dictate the grocery list and give you permission to call the auto shop he recommends. He doesn't want a partner who thinks. He wants someone who looks good on his arm. If you are a Libra, he's probably your ideal mate. If you are the independent type, be prepared for an onslaught of power plays that makes Scorpio look like a rank amateur.

His motto is, "Do as I say, not as I do." He has the annoying habit of trying to make you feel like a dog he's just saved from the pound and expects the same loyalty and blind devotion in return. Should you manage to pierce his hide and wound his ego, he'll shut himself away in a darkened room and brood. Use the respite to catch a nap.

If You Love One—Capricorn Woman

It's a good thing I was born a woman, or I'd have been a drag queen.

DOLLY PARTON (JANUARY 19)

Every Capricorn woman has a built-in sense of style and social grace. Whether her personality is as outgoing as Dolly Parton, or as coolly reserved as Ava Gardner, her basic character is practical and sensible. She seeks a mate who is strong and ambitious and who plans for the future. Since she appreciates the best things in life, plan to take her to the finest restaurant. Oh, and be sure to bring along your stock portfolio and a copy of your family tree, because if one or the other doesn't push her I'm-so-impressed button, she'll never consider you as a serious match.

Leo may be Queen, but lady Capricorn is pure Diva. She can be as emotional as a Cancer at a pity party or as pushy as an Aries on a power trip. She's so status conscious that she won't plan a vacation until she's checked with her travel agent to see where this year's "in" spot is located. She'll pay a hundred dollars for a hairdo she hates if it's the latest style from the hottest salon in town.

In public, she'll be the model of social demeanor because she's always on the lookout for someone rich and famous to kiss up to. At home, you'll eat in the kitchen and watch TV in the bedroom, because she's afraid you'll get a spot on the tablecloth or wrinkle the fabric on the sofa. She spends a good part of the day walking through the house blowing kisses to all the inanimate objects she so dearly loves.

She's pretentious. She may have been raised under a bridge on the wrong side of the train tracks, but before she consents to meet your friends, she'll expect a rundown of their social standing. She'll look down on the one who's content to own one service station instead of a gas company, and fawn over the one who just got paroled from jail for creative accounting. The former she views as lazy, the latter as inspired.

Capricorn hookers are just as snooty. Mayflower madam Sydney Biddle Barrows and Hollywood madam Heidi Fleiss, who each respectively cornered the market on high-class brothels, were just as selective about their clientele. And just as socially aware of their public. When asked to comment about being busted, Biddle told a reporter, "Never say anything on the phone that you wouldn't want your mother to hear at your trial." When Fleiss was paroled, she headed straight for the plastic surgeon. "I had a lot done," she said. "Lips, ears, eyes, boobs. Being in prison with no skin care really does a number on you."

Yours probably won't be as blindly ambitious, but she will have a definite tendency to embellish the truth if the teatime conversation with friends turns to family stories. Her aunt Maybelle, who's the hog-calling champion of West Virginia, might evolve into a much-revered a cappella singing star of the South.

The lady Goat is as humor-challenged as her male counterpart and will mope for days over any offhanded teasing. Her joke switch is set on dim, and the only time she really smiles is when she's emptying the cookie-jar bank to buy another savings bond.

Romantically, she may swing both ways, but she's not into swinging from the chandelier. However, don't confuse serious with sexless. Capricorn megastar Marlene Dietrich was known as the "love-pirate" for the shocking ease with which she stole spouses and lovers away from their partners.

She expects to be pursued, wooed, and put in the mood, which may get a bit tiresome after five or six years. Tossing a diamond between the sheets is a surefire way to get her to dive in bed. Or, if you aren't rich, make it a granola bar. Capricorn women love little gifts and are always on a diet.

Whether yours is the life of the party or the classic woman-behind-the-man, keeping up appearances and long-term security mean more to a Capricorn woman than either a warm blanket or your warm body.

If You Are One-Born Rotten

Get a sun lamp to keep you looking as if you have just come back from somewhere expensive.

Aristotle Onassis (January 15)

You invented the phrase "politically correct." You want people to believe you are a socially astute, dignified, classically chic success magnet. Actually, you are a dedicated social climber, who knows just enough about manners to eat with a fork and not blow your nose in public. However, you are such an accomplished bullshit artist that you successfully fake your way into the highest social circles.

The quest for power drives you as forcefully as it does cousin Scorpio. However, because your emotional nature is in hibernation, you suffer none of the Scorpion's passionate derailments on the way up the corporate ladder. Your business philosophy is that of the early railroad magnates. Kill what you can't buy off and stay on schedule.

An unusual number of your sign have the same taste in food as your symbolic counterpart—anything and everything. You equate exotic with animal parts that no one else will eat and are famous for inviting family and friends over for a home-cooked meal, then refusing to tell them what that is on their plates. A Capricorn invented the term *chef's surprise.*

You are slow to anger because you consider yourself so superior to the rest of humanity that you rarely lower yourself to hold a two-sided conversation. You disregard any opinion except your own, and the most others can expect is a sour-faced glower and flick of your wrist as you dismiss them as blathering fools for whom you have no time.

You are the late-bloomer of the zodiac. Astrologers kindly say that yours is the sign of reverse aging. What this really means is, as a child you sold tickets when your cat had kittens and played Foreclosure instead of Monopoly. And, when you reach the old folks home, your nickname will be either Baby Jane, because you swish through the halls in your tutu, or Letch, because it's finally dawned on you what playing doctor really meant in fifth grade and you're trying to make up for lost time.

You are so conservative that you are two steps right of survivalist. You think fellow Goat Rush Limbaugh should be president, and you burned your Barry Goldwater campaign button when he publicly announced his support of gays in the military.

Capricorn is the sign of the business tycoon, urban legend, hermit, Pope, and party pooper. Goats also make excellent personal shoppers and self-employed hit men. Ever the traditionalist, the latter subscribes to the work ethic of if you want something done right, do it yourself.

At home you enjoy sitting on your four-thousand-dollar sofa (the one Libra couldn't afford) sipping rare wine and quietly conversing with friends. The facts that you have to strain to hear them over the crackling plastic cover and your bottle of 1969 Thunderbird has a rather piquant flavor doesn't bother you a bit. You are too busy pretending the portrait above the fireplace is your great-great-uncle John, whose blood was so blue he signed the Declaration of Independence with it and no one was the wiser.

You also have the strongest will in the zodiac. The only thing holding you back is yourself. Once you reconcile your emotional needs with your drive to succeed, nothing on Earth can stop you. In an argument, there isn't a sign in the Universe that can top you.

You have little patience for the immature antics of Aries and Sagittarius, and one swift kick of your well-manicured hoof sends these two howling down the mountainside. When belligerent Leo attempts to usurp your authority, you grab it by the scruff of the neck and neatly dropkick it into the next county. Water signs Pisces and Cancer instinctively know who's boss and properly defer to you as head of their Universe. Extremist Scorpio quickly finds itself gasping for breath under the heavy boot of Saturn's truth. Air signs Gemini, Libra, and Aquarius whip themselves into a frenzy of frustrated fury trying to broach your implacable demeanor. You and fellow Earth signs Taurus and Virgo understand each other on a soul level and, therefore, rarely have serious confrontations.

Yours is the philosophy of "No pain no gain." You know there's no such thing as a free ride in life and have the rare gift of foresight, so are prepared to work hard in youth in order to ensure a secure old age. Let the rest of the world waste time and live beyond its means. Years from now when everyone else is eating dog food stew and wearing a mismatched, thrift-store wardrobe, you'll be sailing by on your private yacht, enjoying the fruits of your labors, and thumbing your impeccably tanned nose.

It's ALL Relative—The Capricorn Family

Spare the rod, and spoil the child.

PROVERBS 13.24 (PARAPHRASED)

In a Saturn-ruled household you'll never be sure whether you are living in a family, or enrolled in canine obedience school. You won't be allowed to climb on the furniture, slide down the banister, or appear at the dining room table without a shirt and shoes. A tie is optional.

Your Capricorn parents are doggedly determined to see that you succeed in life. Your mom will send you to modeling school at three, dancing school at four, and enroll you in a romance-language course at six. At five you learned how to write your ABCs in calligraphy.

Dad will let you ride on his shoulders as he walks through his office, so you can get a view from the top early on. The day you are born, he will enroll you in his alma mater, or if he's a self-made Goat, the university of his favorite football team.

Neither is too good at hugging, so you might have to make the first move. Both will grill the friends you bring home with the single-mindedness of a dime-store detective on the trail of a murderer, and few will pass inspection. Goat parents have the irritating habit of picking friends for you from among the children in their casual circle of social acquaintances. The fact that you have nothing in common or hate the little snobs means nothing. Mom and Dad don't remember the kid's name, but they do remember the parents' original Degas.

Don't be surprised if your Capricorn baby's first word is your first name. These babies are born serious and most of them pass by the goo-goo stage and go directly to full-sentence use. A Capricorn toddler will have a definite system for his clothes, toys, and picture books and if it doesn't coincide with yours, you will be the one to acquiesce. Capricorn children are strong-willed, but not prone to temper tantrums.

He or she will simply wear down your will by putting the teddy bear behind the couch where it "lives," one time, or one thousand times, should you move it back to the middle of their bed.

You will seldom need to remind your Capricorn teen to do his or her homework, for Saturn-ruled children like to learn. However, if yours prefers learning how to sneak out of the house at night to go joyriding with his friends, you'll have to put bars on the windows to keep him home. Guide him early toward a positive direction, or he may end up head of the neighborhood street gang, instead of class president.

Like all Earth signs, your Capricorn brother or sister will have a place for everything, and you'd better leave it there. Until you ask permission. They on the other hand will tell you that they are borrowing your coat, or your car, in midaction. The double standard will be irritating, but push back too hard and you'll find yourself doing double chore duty, because the Goat told Mom and Dad that she has to study extra hard for a nonexistent test.

How do you survive? Put your head down and plod right beside them. Practice your French, fluff up your angora sweater, and make sure your shoes shine. The day after graduation, you can pack up your troubles in your Gucci luggage and tap-dance your way down the road.

Office Party—Bitches, Snitches, and the Chronically Inert

When the president does it that means it's not illegal.
RICHARD M. NIXON (JANUARY 9)

Every Capricorn boss is a distant relative of Simon Legree. He or she keeps one eye on the clock, the other on your hunched back, and an ear to the wall in order to catch you making a personal telephone call.

This boss will walk by your desk five minutes before quitting time to make sure you haven't left early. If you tell her that she is driving you to a nervous breakdown, she will tell you to do it on your lunch hour, that report you're working on has to be out by five.

Boss Goat's office looks like it won a best-pretentious-display award from the Association of Pompous Windbags. Her desk will be a monstrosity of the most endangered wood money can buy and she will still use an old-fashioned intercom to summon you, because it feeds her sense of self-importance.

His management style is driven ambition. His office looks like his home, because he spends more time there. Help him land that billion-dollar deal and the most you can expect is a mumbled "Good job." In his mind, he's solely responsible for his success and you are only another one of his tools, like his cell phone.

Capricorn coworkers are quiet, hardworking, and inconspicuous. They can be friendly and shy, or reserved and aloof, but you'll never see one goofing off by the water cooler with Aries or gossiping on the phone like Gemini. A dedicated Goat has no time to waste. You can bet that any Capricorn who has worked for the same company for more than ten years has steadily worked his or her way right up through the rank and file. All Goats have the same agenda, to keep gaining power and status.

The good news is that, unless your job is directly in his or her way, and there's no alternate route that won't set back their personal timetable, you have little to worry about. The bad news is that if your position is the next step up to the ivory tower, you had better either polish up your résumé or prepare for a long, unrelenting struggle. You can keep a Goat at bay, but you will have to work longer and harder, give up your lunch hours, and quit e-mailing your friends when you should be balancing the budget. There are some boulders a mountain Goat can't maneuver, but unless he or she finds an equally acceptable alternate route, you can expect your chair to be repeatedly butted for a long time.

Irking a Capricorn is fun and easy. Act like working is the most fun you've ever had. Joke with your coworkers as you speed-file your correspondence, talk on the phone, take extra time at lunch, and spend time flirting with the Libra in the next cubicle. Deliberate, cautious Capricorn will pull in his horns, shoot you a black look, and harrumph his way out the door.

Cn't We ALL Get ALong?

So how can you possibly stand living with this grumpy tight-wad? Easy, once you know the way to his or her heart.

Penny-pinching Goats

Every Capricorn has the reputation of still having the first dollar he or she earned. That may be true, but the Goat is shrewd rather than stingy. No matter how meager your income, your Goat will always manage to pay the bills, sock some in the retirement account, and buy a new pair of designer shoes. Your home will be full of light and flowers and uncluttered by bargain-basement furniture and cheap artwork.

Capricorns believe in quality versus quantity. Yours will prefer sleeping on a futon while saving for the antique bedroom set you both want. When you do have the price, he or she will negotiate a discount. Goats believe in clipping coupons, buying in bulk, and purchasing the same designer suit in three different colors when they go on sale. They also abhor wastefulness, so plan on eating lots of leftovers and adding water to that last ounce of hair conditioner. Plan, too, to retire ten years earlier than the average person and to dine on filet mignon while your friends eat hamburger.

Social-Climbing Goats

Capricorn is the most determined sign in the zodiac. Whether yours is a megamogul closing another deal or a cubicle dweller seeking a promotion, all Goats are goal oriented. And they all respect the people who have reached their goals. Since they are also practical, Goats see no value in schmoozing a thirty-year veteran of the secretarial pool when they could be getting a few pointers on the best way to formulate the presentation that might land them a corner office. This has nothing to do with social climbing and everything to do with laying a foundation for a secure future, which includes you.

Goats respond very well to social obligation, so remind yours that a moment or two spent conversing with the staff is expected. He or she may grouse and shuffle off to say hi to the new office boy standing by himself in the corner. Don't be surprised if your Goat fairly skips back to your side, beaming because Saturn has rewarded his sense of duty with another opportunity. Turns out, that kid is the boss's son and your Goat is the only person in the room who bothered to stop and chat.

Cold-Hearted Goats

Of all misconceptions surrounding Capricorn, the biggest one is that they are cold hearted, emotionally distant, and overbearing. They all have these traits, but no more so than the rest of the zodiac. The Goat's basic character is reserved, even painfully shy, and all have an abject fear of making fools of themselves in public. This is one reason they don't take practical jokes or teasing well. They feel victimized, not amused.

This shy reserve often carries over into the romance department. In general, Goats tend to marry later than other signs because they realize how serious is the search for a lasting relationship. After so many years of carefully crafting a brick wall around their emotions, it's naturally going to take you a bit of time to chip it away. Capricorns love the trappings of romance. Wine, candlelight, music, dinner for two beneath the moon—all set a mood yours can't resist. They also have a very tactile sense, so investing in a pair of silk sheets or matching velour bathrobes is a sure way to get the attention you seek. As for that "reverse aging" part, you can count on your Capricorn to be living proof in the bedroom.

Gloomy Goats

All Goats have a pessimistic streak. Whether your Goat's is pencil thin or as wide as the Mississippi, it will seem like he or she frequently walks around muttering how harsh life is and worrying about whether to go on vacation or save the money in case the car breaks down.

There's no escaping the Saturnine traits of stern discipline and self-denial. That's one reason young Goats often become workaholics while the rest of their friends are enjoying the freedom of single-hood. However, opportunity often follows Capricorn, probably as a reward for a diligent nature.

Assure yours that the roof won't cave in while you're in Hawaii and that even if it does, thanks to his or her astute negotiation, your homeowner's all-purpose, all-event coverage insurance policy would pay all damages. Next, compliment your Cappy on the skill with which he or she snapped up that two-for-one ten-day cruise and the diligence it took to keep checking the cabin reservations until they noticed a last-minute cancellation for the owner's suite. Wrap up your pep talk by noting how much money all this conscientious attention has saved. So much, in fact, that you can not only take extra spending cash on the trip but also add to the children's college fund. Have a great time in the islands.

Quick Tips for Emergencies

- ♑ Goats need financial security.
- ♑ Reserved good manners are key to getting their attention.
- ♑ Goats appreciate practical discussion to emotional argument.

♑ Bring out their romantic side with soft music and candlelight.

♑ Gaslight them by treating work like play and play like work.

Top Goats and Goat-getters

Idi Amin
Benedict Arnold
Reverend Jim Bakker
Hermann Göring
Gypsy Rose Lee
Linda Lovelace
Marilyn Manson
Bert Parks
Soupy Sales
J. D. Salinger

Chapter Twelve

Aquarius

January 20–February 18

Mama Was a Spy;
Daddy Was a Psychopath

Element: Air. Aquarius Air is electrically charged and unpredictable. You know the storm is coming; you just aren't sure when or with what force.

Quality: Fixed. Aquarius is the human version of the tornado that carried Dorothy to Oz.

Symbol: The Water Bearer. Deluge. Flood. Pour-forth.

Ruler: Uranus, the god of abrupt change, and Saturn, the god of repression and status quo.

Favorite Pastime: Getting in someone's face.

Favorite Book: *Channeling Dead House Pets for Fun and Profit.*

Role Model: Goldfinger.

Dream Job: Head borg.

Key Phrase: "Resistance is futile."

Body Part: Ankles, permanently twisted from spinning on their heels and marching out of the room.

Approach with Caution

Aquarius, the eleventh sign of the zodiac, lives in the House of Friendship, Intellect, and Idealism. Kind astrology describes the Water Bearer as an assertive, original, and idealistic individualist who treats every person equally. What you get is an in-your-face eccentric who spouts assorted oddball ideologies to anyone he or she can corner.

Next to Scorpio, more Aquarians check in and out of the local nut farm than any other sign. Personality Disorder was coined for the Aquarian head case. As we are now officially in the Age of Aquarius, you may notice a marked increase in the agitation factor of your favorite Water Bearer. Get used to it. They are going to be going over the edge in droves during the next millennium.

Aquarius is dual-ruled by Uranus and Saturn. Uranus, the planet of abrupt change, brings the revolution. Saturn, the planet of dogma and repression, indicates the status quo. In Aquarius these two heavy hitters create an unpredictable personality torn between creating change and craving security. Water Bearers try to force the world to change around them in order to create an illusion of nonconformity. In reality, they fear change.

Aquarians are aloof, not passionate. This is because they fear that introspection will reveal that they really don't have all the answers. Aquarians chase the future instead of living in the present. Being born without the self-analysis gene has created a schism between having a keen judgment about others, but little understanding of themselves. Disagree with the Aquarian version of truth, and risk never seeing them again. Prove that they are as self-deluded as the rest of us, and they will shatter like the thinnest glass.

If You Love One—Aquarius Man

Start the day with a smile, and get it over with.
W. C. Fields (January 29)

If he isn't actually brilliant, an Aquarius male will be at least an innovative thinker who envisions a wonderful future and usually finds a way to make it real. His delightfully spontaneous side will prefer unplanned treks to out-of-the-way places; his practical, respectable side makes him secure and stable. He reads books, is concerned for the environment, and will simultaneously be your best friend and decidedly unconventional lover. Think you see a romantic breath of fresh air heading your way? That panting you hear crashing through the underbrush belongs to a cross between Drs. Strangelove and Frankenstein.

At best, he is an arbitrary, irritable eccentric who lives inside his own head, but is overall fairly harmless. At worst, he's a cold-blooded, cheerfully vile monster who will subject you to endless mental tortures, then watch you crumble with the emotional separation of a psychopath. He may have as caustic a tongue as W. C. Fields, who called his famous Leo co-star Mae West "a plumber's idea of Cleopatra." Or live for years, looking and acting as normal as anyone else, then go out for milk one day and disappear.

A male Water Bearer has delusions of grandeur that would shame a Leo. He fancies himself as the world's savior, whether or not the world wants saving. And he will not hesitate if he must to force his plans for change upon an unsuspecting group.

Consider Aquarian president Franklin Delano Roosevelt, whose grandiose scheme for relieving both a suffering economy and millions of unemployed Americans included the New Deal. Social Security Tax, Social Welfare, and the World War II Victory (Income) Tax all sprang from his vision.

Whether you agree or disagree with his political views, Roosevelt cannot be faulted for his humanitarian attempt to help the masses. However, in typical Aquarius fashion, the plan had little detail or built-in restriction so it laid the foundation for the tangled mess we have today. Like the good Dr. Frankenstein, his intent was to restore life, but the result was an uncontrollable monster.

The Water Bearer is neither selfish nor domineering, but that's only because you will see less of this man than a Sagittarius traveling salesman. He won't physically leave home because his trips are all in his mind. But he will virtually live in the garage or basement tinkering with his latest invention, trying to contact alien life forces, or calling the FBI and offering his services as master spy.

He is Fixed Air, and like his cousins Leo, Taurus, and Scorpio, he doesn't play well with others. He is as obstinate, tenacious, and attention seeking as those guys, but he's also ingenious at mind games. It was probably an Aquarius male who caused the legal system to devise the term *mental cruelty*.

He's twitchy. Most male Water Bearers have a nervous grimace that people mistake for a lopsided grin. His electrically charged personality makes him the king of snap judgments, endless pronouncements, and long answers to questions you never asked. On especially wild days his mere appearance causes dogs to howl and cats to hiss.

He may be into substance abuse—not to delude himself as Pisces does, but to simply calm him enough to hold a job. And the amount he can take and still function under would put any other sign in a coma.

He's paranoid. He will keep the curtains closed, the TV tuned to CNN, and the answering machine in action. He will expect you to report any unusual activities at the grocery store, or on your job, which he will immediately assimilate into his latest disaster fantasy. He will frequently hold conversations with the person standing three feet behind you, the one only he can see.

Although he loves to roam around the house naked as a lover, he prefers a good book, unless you capture his attention by appealing to his perverse side. The more bizarre you look and act, the better he likes it. Pretending that silver buckle you're wearing is really a tiny nuclear weapon, which may or may not detonate the exact instant he does, will drive him into a sexual frenzy. Strap it around *his* waist, tell him he's the ultimate sex machine, and you will be set for a night of multiple pleasures.

He's inventive, original, and, when in balance with his Saturn nature, an unstoppable force. Consider original shock rocker Aquarian Alice Cooper. True to the Uranus-ruled side of his nature, he allegedly took his stage name from a seventeenth-century witch who spoke to him via the Ouija board. Of his band he said, "We were into fun, sex, death and money . . . and we drove a stake right through the heart of the Love Generation."

Cooper's wild-eyed expression, fright-night hair and makeup, and onstage penchant for flaming objects and gruesome theatrics such as mock hangings, guillotining, and murder of infant dolls that gush blood, all in the name of good fun, is vintage Aquarius. And as any true Water Bearer, he believes his job is to leave his audience feeling like they were "at the greatest party they were ever at in their lives."

His offstage life merges nicely with the Saturn side of the Aquarian nature. Cooper has been married to the same woman for twenty years, has three children, coaches Little League and soccer, is an avid golfer, and raises more than $150,000 a year for charity.

Whether yours is a weird-but-harmless genius or a sarcastic anarchist, life with the Aquarian male is as wild a ride as you can get on planet Earth.

If You Love One-Aquarius Woman

You can have your titular recognition. I'll take money and power.
HELEN GURLEY BROWN (FEBRUARY 18)

She's a free spirit who is eternally curious and always friendly. An Aquarian woman will enchant you with her enigmatic charm and seeks a man who is both romantic and intellectual. She is neither possessive nor jealous and believes that love begins with friendship. She is also a total individual who marches to her own drummer. Whether this is the beat of a jazz band or a set of tom-toms as she stakes you out on the nearest anthill is something you should try to determine before the wedding.

The good news is that she is one of the nicest people in the Universe. The bad news is, that's because she always does exactly what she pleases. An Aquarius female is rebellious, headstrong, and contrary. She can be selfishly independent and exasperating, especially when she is running through the house screaming, "Freedom!"

When angry, she can act out in an aggressive, childish way. She may stamp her feet, order you out of the house, or even trash the place in a fit of petulant indignation. But, usually, she approaches anger from the same detached mental perspective as she does everything else in life, preferring to argue and provoke you into a rage. As all Air signs, she is easily bored and delights in stirring the pot, especially if she thinks it will piss you off.

She's so unpredictable that each time you kiss her good-bye, you'll never know who, or what, will greet you when you return. She has few inhibitions. Some female Water Bearers have green hair, purple hair, or no hair at all. She will wear a nose ring, a toe ring, or six earrings in one ear and a tongue stud. She will dress any way she fancies, no matter what the occasion, and is apt to wear Levi's and a "Free Tibet" T-shirt to a formal dinner, where she will not hesitate to discuss any topic under the sun, including death, politics, cannibalism, or cannibalizing dead politicians. Her personality is combination shock treatment and rugged individualism.

The female Water Bearer loves gossip as much as Cousin Gemini. However, her odd curiosity lends itself to ferreting out the most disgusting bits of information she can find to horrify you with as she unleashes her maniacal laughter. She will also keep you up all night analyzing such inane topics as how dust bunnies are formed and whether or not Cancer Alex Trebek is really an android.

She has a horde of friends of all ages, sexes, persuasions, and character types. And she will be available any time of the day or night for guidance counseling, a free meal, or a warm bed. If you want to win her heart, be prepared to feel as if you are living in a combination bus station and therapist's office.

The more bizarre you are, the better your chances of getting her in the sack. Tell her you are doing research on vampire sexual rites in Los Angeles, and she'll confess that she channels new positions for the Kama Sutra from Bela Lugosi. Pretend you are an alien sex fiend from the planet Halcyon and she will wrap herself in Christmas lights and fall at your feet. However, unless you are an Aries with an endless imagination, or a Scorpio who can appeal to her perverse side, you'll soon find yourself with a bored partner who prefers reading about sex to doing the deed. But, don't confuse bored with non-sexy.

Hollywood bombshell Aquarius Mamie Van Doren wore the bullet bra when Leo Madonna was wearing diapers, and Mamie rarely, if ever, confused a good lay with a romantic attachment. True to the clever Aquarian nature, she survived the Blond Bimbo era of Hollywood, the sixties, and is still going strong. She still loves men, and as she's fond of saying, "Mamie likes 'em young."

Aquarius is not into blatant emotionalism, so if you are worship-needy like Leo, or a drama-drenched Water sign, you'll soon feel like you've stumbled through an electrically charged whirlwind and been zapped, snapped, and spit out as too stupid to deal with, all in record time.

Ms. Aquarius also has a touch of money grubber in her soul. Although she's not quite as obvious as a Capricorn checking your Dun and Bradstreet rating, she does firmly believe in the old cliché that says it's as easy to love a rich person as a poor one. Charming, stunning, and nine-time-married Zsa Zsa Gabor once said, "I've never hated a man enough to give back his diamonds."

Gabor's guest role on the last show of the old *Batman* TV series was typical of the Aquarius female. Maybe that's why she remembers it so fondly. Zsa Zsa played Minerva, an evil woman who owned a spa for men, where she scanned their brains under special hair dryers. "I loved the character," Gabor said. "The wardrobe was all gaudy and silver, and nothing can be more exciting than that. These hair dryers got all the spy stories out of the people's brains. One person was a jewelry salesman and I could find out the combination to his safe. I opened that safe and diamonds kept on falling all over me. I loved it."

The title of her autobiography, *One Lifetime Is Not Enough,* sums up the philosophy of every Aquarian woman, including yours.

If You Are One—Born Rotten

"I'm Aquarius—destined for greatness, or madness."

HAIR (A ROCK OPERA)

You have the annoying habit of acting like an authority on subjects about which you know little or nothing. This is because your brain is like an encyclopedia with chunks of pages missing. You confuse snatches of a conversation held a year ago with the Adventure Channel's special on the pyramids you saw last week. Then insist you had a conversation with the curator of an Egyptian museum on the relics found in King Tut's tomb. The sad part is that you believe your fantasy so you are not only a phony but also a fruitcake.

Aliens kidnap Aquarians more often than any other sign. In fact, you probably are an alien who uses the kidnapped story as a cover for your strange behavior patterns. Your brain works faster than you can speak, so your conversation is riddled with mispronounced five-syllable words that makes you sound like Roger Rabbit talking about his uncle's "probate" gland.

You have a great sympathy for the trials and tribulations of humanity. Of course you rarely do anything other than expound on how much you care as you are too busy bugging your neighbor's house because you are convinced she is hiding five of the ten Most Wanted list in her basement. In fact, *America's Most Wanted* is your favorite TV show and you know every operator by name.

Aquarius is the sign of the humanitarian, inventor, mad scientist, and anarchist. Water Bearers also make good hippies, cross-dressers, and dyslexic English professors. You all own original cast recordings of *Hair* and keep your valuables locked in the safe disguised as an Early American end table in your den.

Your never-ending quirkiness and incessant questioning are the reasons why you have no close friends and your family members all live in other states. This is fine with you because it gives you the opportunity to scope out the action on the Greyhound to Phoenix. Besides, you love a captive audience and the trip gives you a chance to entertain your newly found friends with your ability to play "Yankee Doodle" with your armpits.

You have a kinship with the bizarre and collect items like petrified bat guano and that black stuff you find under the porch in humid weather. You are curious about strange religious movements or offbeat psychic practices such as Navel Lint Reading.

You are so unconcerned with what other people think of you that you rarely bother to bathe or dress on weekends. If an unexpected visitor arrives at your front door and is offended by your body odor and cluttered house, you figure it serves them right for not calling ahead so you could tell them to stay home.

In love, you are very selective. As soon as you realize your newest prospect is a poster child for the criminally insane, you are hooked. However, since you have no idea of how to sustain romance, as fast as the lust wanes, or the handcuffs break, you are merrily on your way in search of newer and weirder conquests. When it comes to marriage, the most your spouse can hope for is a divorce.

You are the most annoying sign in the zodiac. You force friends and family alike to all-night speculations about the pros and cons of stamps you lick versus the peel-and-stick kind. However, you don't really understand how anything works and your scientific knowledge comes from watching programs like *Bill Nye the Science Guy.* You think fellow Aquarian Jerry Springer's show is a good example of a fun look at real life. The fact that he's picked people so unaware that they don't realize they are being ridiculed makes you laugh all the harder.

You are also the world's most original thinker. You are sensible, friendly, and idealistic. Your fierce need for independence, however, can be a dual-edged sword. Learn to overcome the urge to lay down the law and spout ultimatums before getting the facts straight, and you'll have the rest of the zodiac eating out of your hand. In the meantime, as a verbal gunslinger, you're the fastest draw in the Universe.

When Earth signs Capricorn and Virgo try to pick apart your dreams, you cut a tornado's swath through their insecure characters. Your razor-edged observation about the Bull's hypocritical nature stops a charging Taurus in his tracks. Theatrical manipulators Cancer and Pisces disintegrate in the face of your tell-it-like-it-is candor. Your ability to coolly ignore Scorpio's obsession for control sends them into a frenzy of self-destruction. Fire signs Aries and Sagittarius burn themselves out when pitted against the force of your electric personality. And you squelch Leo's egotistical posturing with a few succinct observations of their self-centered nature. You and fellow Air signs Gemini and Libra understand each other on a soul level and, therefore, rarely have serious confrontations.

Your philosophy is "Honesty is the best policy." You are a free spirit who couldn't care less about conforming to society's standards. And you understand that home is a state of mind, not a defined place. Let other people cling to their outworn beliefs and nine-to-five routines. Years from now when your detractors are sitting in the clubhouse of their gated community, living vicariously through cable TV and canned music, you can send them a video of you and the Dalai Lama discussing the true path to enlightenment.

It's ALL Relative—The Aquarius Family

"I'm crazy, you're crazy, we're all crazy."

Alice Cooper (February 4)

An Aquarian home is part homeless shelter and part science fiction movie. Strange people lurk in the bushes, the phone rings constantly, and the power company sends your folks a gift basket every Christmas because your house looks like the Electric Light Parade.

Your mom will have a drive-through window in the kitchen where she hands out banana sandwiches to the hungry. Your dad will have three cell phones listed under assumed names, and a basement lab to rival Mr. Freeze. He'll expect you to gather information on your schoolteachers for the Education Manifesto he plans to write.

Your home will be decorated with ancient Babylonian religious objects and littered with books on topics such as obscure inventions, alien abductions, and the history of circus sideshows. However, both parents will be great listeners, and very little you can do will shock them.

When asked about his indulgence regarding his children, who kept pet goats in the White House, Aquarius dad Abraham Lincoln said, "It is my pleasure that my children are free, happy, and unrestrained by parental tyranny."

Your parents will absolutely insist on total honesty. Lying to this Mom and Dad could land you in a homeless shelter down by the bus station. Neither parent will stop you from choosing your own path in life. In fact they will be eager to kick you out the door as soon as you blow out the candles on your eighteenth birthday cake. They plan to turn your bedroom into a shelter for runaway circus midgets.

The only thing predictable about an Aquarius child is his or her unpredictability. As a baby, your little Water Bearer will be sweet and docile. It's when they become toddlers that you will need to exercise caution. Water Bearer children are extremely prone to losing things and having accidents because they are always daydreaming.

Aquarian teens wear Pendleton shirts over aqua-colored tights to school, dye their hair black, red, and yellow all within the same week, and have a diverse circle of friends that includes the grade-schooler next door and the elderly greeter at the local megamart. When other kids are dreaming of prom night, young Water Bearers are figuring out how to rewire the fire alarm so it rings every half hour all evening.

Aquarius siblings are forgetful. They will enlist your aid in searching for their car keys, homework, and the family cat they let escape because they were wondering where they left their sunglasses instead of watching the door. They are just as liable to forget you at the movies or the mall, so make sure you take your cell phone or change to call your parents. They are definitely quirky, but usually harmless. They won't beat you up, like a Taurus, or get in your face like Aries. They won't sob at a sideways look, like Cancer, or fight over bathroom time like Libra. In fact, they probably won't remember you are related unless you keep introducing yourself.

Your folks may be the neighborhood oddballs, but the education you receive at home will be ten times more enlightening and a hundred times more interesting than anything you'll ever learn from academia.

Surviving in a family of eccentric Aquarians will simultaneously try your patience and test your embarrassment factor. But, by the time you're ready to leave for college, you will have learned the subtle difference between telling an outright lie and omitting pertinent facts to save a friend from jail, the real scoop on Area 51, and how to organize a protest march.

Office Party-Bitches, Snitches, and the Chronically Inert

I have not failed. I've just found ten thousand ways it won't work.

Thomas Edison (February 11)

Having an Aquarius boss is like watching one of those theatrical double-faced masks spin. First he, or she, will retreat into the executive suite and refuse all calls, then dash out and dump a last-minute, completely off-the-wall project in your lap that has to be finished by quitting time. Asking for guidance won't help because he won't have any idea of how to manage the details. That's your job. You will be expected to complete it fast, accurately, and without grumping, or you can expect to be coolly and quickly dropped from the employment roster.

Your Aquarius boss has the aggravating habit of talking at, instead of to, you. Go to her office, pad and pencil in hand, and you will scribble for an hour trying to make sense of the convoluted and contradictory statements she's spouting faster than a speed-talking champion. Interrupt to ask for clarification on what recarpeting her office has to do with developing a new marketing plan to install ice cream stands in the Sahara, and you'll find yourself on the receiving end of a look that will make you feel like a lab rat caught in a maze. She wasn't giving instructions; she was just thinking aloud. Aquarian bosses do everything aloud.

According to history, Water Bearer Charles Darwin's "Flow of conversation . . . would often go off on a tangent this way, then another tangent that way, in whatever topic he was discussing."

Aquarian coworkers are too busy climbing the company grapevine to worry about climbing the corporate ladder. That old joke about clock-in, take a break, greet coworkers, go to lunch, read the mail, take a break, phone friends and family, cancel a meeting and clock-out is a perfect description of the typical Aquarian work day.

If a Water Bearer does set his sights on your position, he will most likely just tell you that he can do a better job and you should start looking for a transfer for the good of the company. Being the humanitarian he is, he will offer to write you a letter of reference. He'll also start schmoozing the boss and rewrite a blended job description for both your positions to prove he can save the company the amount of your salary and benefits.

To foil him, simply announce that the research department has detected faint-but-audible signals emanating from deep within the earth and aimed at the Andromeda Galaxy. Even when he discovers your hoax, he will be so intrigued with the idea that he'll stop trying to get your job and invite you to lunch to discuss your inspired psychic insight and a plan to prove that you are right.

Can't We All Get Along?

Afraid that you will short out if you attempt to snuggle up to this human lightning bolt? Don't be. Grounding them is easy if you know where to redirect that unpredictable Uranian energy.

Overamped Water Bearers

Aquarians are born with an erratic nature and a highly charged personality. They frequently suffer insomnia due to their overworked thought processes and become testy, depressed, and physically exhausted. Keep yours from short-circuiting by making sure they get regular exercise and plenty of rest. When your Aquarian complains that the TV's too loud and the light's too bright, it's time to unplug the boob tube and the telephone, reset the dimmer switch, and hand him or her a book on yoga and a few meditation tapes. Calcium-magnesium tablets help to reduce nervous tension when taken regularly.

Detached Water Bearers

Aquarians are friendly, open-minded, and fun loving. On the surface, they embrace everyone with tolerance sans prejudice. When it comes to deeper emotional feelings, they are often ambivalent and reserved. This is because Water Bearers use frivolity to avoid confronting their own feelings. They feast on intellectual stimulation but fear emotional attachment.

Helping them to develop compassion for the individual as well as the cause will ground their humanitarian efforts in realism. Take yours to the soup kitchen and let him serve the homeless. Or to the animal shelter to help organize the filing system.

Once they refine their objective observations with emotional awareness, their character will take a quantum leap forward. And you can watch for a cost-saving, streamlined process to feed triple the number of hungry humans in your city. Or an in-depth revision of the process of animal adoption that spares the lives of thousands of innocent pets.

Unpredictable Water Bearers

Aquarius is the most independent sign. Your Water Bearer is capable of buying a new car, or a new house, or accepting a job in another country, all without consulting you. And then be genuinely perplexed by your anger. Their hearts are in the right place. Their methods are wildly frustrating.

Since Water Bearers appreciate truth and readily acknowledge their mistakes, they will appreciate an honest discussion. Emotional displays designed to produce guilt won't work. Stick to the facts, and present them as calmly and rationally as you can. Normally, this works quite well. However, if yours is too dogmatic, you can appeal to their sense of loyalty, and ask that they at least leave a note the next time they leave for Africa.

Temperamental Water Bearers

Aquarians chafe against structure and routine. School, work, and home life can all become too confining for their inquisitive and social natures. A bored, restless Water Bearer can be appallingly rebellious, touchy, and contrary. They are perfectly capable of starting a minor, or major, riot, depending on how long they've been forced to act normal.

Whether it's an outrageous wardrobe, the study of an extinct civilization, or a basement laboratory, every Aquarian needs a way to vent a strong need for individualism. Your unwavering support in allowing yours to be as offbeat as possible, within the obvious laws of work and school, helps them succeed and retain their independence. At home, let the kids decorate their rooms as wildly as they want and your significant other wear a coat hanger antenna on his or her head if that's what pleases them. Who knows, you may be the first house on the block to contact life on another planet.

Quick Tips for Emergencies

≈ Water Bearers need lots of space.
≈ Hands-on charity work helps develop compassion.

≋ Get your way with honesty and a rational, factual argument.

≋ They love unexpected or unusual gifts.

≋ Gaslight them by telling them that you just saw a flying saucer.

Wicked and Wired Water Bearers

Eva Braun
Aaron Burr
Lewis Carroll
E.T.
Dan Quayle
Grigori Rasputin
Ronald Reagan
Arlen Specter
The Sixties
Wolfman Jack

Chapter Thirteen

Pisces

February 19–March 20

Welcome, to the Twilight Zone

Element: Water. Pisces Water is unrestrained. A quiet ocean looks inviting and harmless. Wade out too far, and you'll be caught in an undertow of treacherous currents and swept away.

Quality: Mutable. Fish never know whether they are coming or going.

Symbol: The Fishes. Fishy. Bottom feeders. Piranha. Sharks.

Ruler: Neptune, the god of flimflam and desert mirages.

Favorite Hobby: Mixing over-the-counter medications to test their hallucinogenic affects.

Favorite Book: *The Sedona Guide to Interplanetary Communication.*

Role Model: Mr. Bill.

Dream Job: Professional mourner.

Key Phrase: "I'm so confused."

Body Part: The feet. Suffers fallen arches from running away from life.

Approach with Caution

Pisces, the twelfth and last sign of the zodiac, resides in the House of Sorrows, Secrets, and Self-undoing. Astrology books customarily paint Pisces as visionary, imaginative, and intro-spective souls who have a natural, empathetic understanding of the human condition. Scrape off the gloss and you'll find a reality-challenged dreamer who is gullible, disorganized, chronically distraught, and totally helpless.

Neptune, the god of illusion, rules Pisces and bestows a naive, escapist personality. Fish walk through life with tunnel vision and a pair of blinders for good measure. Every action is filtered through the Pisces version of cheesecloth. Any nasty lumps of truth are simply caught and disposed of. This makes Pisces loser-magnets. They smell like free lunch and gas money. Fish get dumped on more than any other sign. But that's OK with them because it's the only time anyone notices them. They tolerate everything, because they can't figure out how to do anything about it.

Fish are resistant, not realistic. The fear of change grounds Pisces. It negates their creativity and ability to follow their dreams to a successful conclusion. Pisces prefer the status quo, even if it's detrimental, to risking the unknown. Being born without the I-deserve-it gene has left them at the mercy of their own escapist nature. Argue your point and the Fish slips into a state of rote agreement. Prove your argument and Pisces simply retreats into a convenient world of fantasy.

If You Love One-Pisces Man

If I'm to be a chauvinist pig, I want to be number one pig.
Bobby Riggs (February 25)

He's a dreamboat who lives for romance, and his hypnotic charisma will leave you weak-kneed and breathless. He may be a visionary like Copernicus, or a joker à la Billy Crystal, but a Pisces man is intuitive, caring, and sympathetic. No other male in the Universe is as capable of profound love and devotion. Unfortunately, he's so in love with himself that you don't stand a chance.

The male Fish is the emotional black hole of the Universe. Toss your heart, soul, and car keys, and all will disappear forever. This guy learned at an appalling young age how to weasel his way out of work and charm his way into bed.

He's definitely sensual, sexy, and cute, in a debauched sort of way. Don't let the façade fool you. At home he may be a quiet little Fish, swimming around and around the beer bottle, but romantically he is the great white shark of the zodiac. A Scorpio man will hurt you because he has a morbid fear of rejection. Your Pisces guy will do it just to keep his teeth sharpened.

He's a natural born liar. And he's honed the art until he fools himself. Such as when he's perched on his favorite bar stool, watching the sports channel and ogling hot bodies, but telling himself he's gathering material for the novel he plans to write. The only thing this loser will ever write is a smeared phone number on his cocktail napkin.

He's self-destructive. Pisces Desi Arnaz had everything. Looks, career, and for its time, a state-of-the-art TV show with wife, Leo Lucille Ball. Arnaz possessed the extraordinary talent for both creative artistry and business acumen. He also possessed the extraordinary Piscean thirst for alcohol, and roving eye, which ultimately left Ball no choice but to divorce him. Ball became a megastar. Arnaz battled alcohol and obscurity for the rest of his life.

He loves sex games. Feel free to wear your nurse's uniform but expect him to play patient, not doctor. Buy a dog collar and he will bark. Introduce him to your best friend if you dare, but don't leave them alone. He will have affairs anywhere, any time, with anyone who will hold still long enough. And with an icy detachment that rivals his Gemini cousin. The Fish can leave you full of his declarations of undying love, drive straight to his favorite watering hole, and pick up the first available body.

Or, full of his divine spiritual fervor, à la Pisces Jimmy Swaggart, hop in his Caddy and head for the nearest hooker. In classic Pisces self-delusion, when caught with his parables down, Swaggart blamed the woman for being a minion of the Devil who tempted him to stray. Then, he gave one of the most spectacular public displays of improvised remorse and Emmy-caliber acting since the night female Fish, Tammy Faye Bakker, ripped off her false eyelashes on TV to prove that she wasn't afraid to reveal her real self. Can you say Amen?

Don't expect your Fish to be the breadwinner. Some Pisces males start on a career path early, but if yours hasn't dropped the remote and picked up a degree by the time he's in his late twenties, forget it. You will end up with a ne'er-do-well who thinks making his fortune means winning the lottery, and that Real TV is culturally educational. If you are a Virgo with a job, house, and checkbook, or a Cancer who doesn't mind playing nursemaid for the rest of your life, this guy was meant for you.

He's tedious. He has a compulsion to use the same clichés he's used since high school and will invariably run a subject straight into the ground in the shortest possible time. Telling him he's not funny only eggs him on, because he's not after your laughter, he's out to provoke you.

All bluff and no substance, Mr. Fish is a cast of thousands and even he doesn't know what scene he'll play next. But, since he does like role-playing you could pretend you're the Lone Ranger and ride on.

If You Love One-Pisces Woman

Yo, are you trying to play me? Trust me, honey, you don't want to go there.

QUEEN LATIFAH (MARCH 18)

She has an aura of responsiveness that instantly puts you at ease. The female Pisces is a classic romantic who expects her mate to be a gentle man. She prefers privacy to partying, quality to quantity, and you, alone, to the rest of the world. Consider yourself the luckiest man alive? What if I told you that her zodiac nickname is Queen of the Horizontal Mamba, and that her commitment to you won't necessarily slow her down?

Ms. Pisces is as sexually diffuse as Fish-boy, except where the male tricks his lovers into believing he is a prince in a frog's clothing, she tricks herself that every man she gets between the sheets, or on top of the Xerox machine, is her One True Love, at least for a couple of hours. This woman has kissed dozens of toads in her quest for a soul mate. Trouble is, she rarely lifts her eyes higher than the swamp. Of course, this is extremely lucky for you if you are demented, unemployable, a hopeless mama's boy, or an escaped felon.

Her basic personality is like a metaphorical aquarium where a great variety of fish jostle for position. Dangle your fingers over the tank and you'll never be sure whether a gentle dolphin will raise its back to be petted, or Jaws will snap them off for lunch. Angry Fish spout like Moby Dick blasting steam, then dive for the nearest dark place. She will become visibly agitated if you press her, and can snap off a few sarcastic remarks. However, she will most likely just shriek and dissolve into a hysterical, sobbing heap.

At first you'll adore the lavish attention she offers. Soon, though, you'll get a distinct tight-in-the-chest feeling when she begins to nag. And the Pisces female has honed the art of nagging to the level of Chinese water torture. She will prod and push, trying to mold you into her ideal mate. Trouble is, she has not a clue as to who that person is. All female Fish idealize Daddy, especially if he doesn't deserve it, and apply this same irrational logic to you. It has nothing to do with heroes and everything to do with distancing herself from a truly intimate relationship.

A Pisces woman may appear fragile, helpless, and otherworldly. However, beneath that innocent smile is a spine of stainless steel. Consider Elizabeth Taylor, the famous Pisces astrologers love to use as an example of an exotic, delicate Fish. Taylor has survived dozens of operations, several near-death experiences, and brain surgery. Her health issues alone would have killed a lesser person years ago, not to mention her romantic stamina in the marriage arena. In addition to multiple divorces and widowhood, she's survived two marriages to the same Scorpio, Richard Burton. You call that fragile?

Ms. Fish is her own worst enemy, and prefers self-pity to rational discussion. Argue with her and she will either turn the air blue with language so foul it would make a sailor blush, or fling herself upon the nearest piece of furniture and sob her guts out. It won't take you long to figure out that she's hooked on drama and actually likes a good fight. It gives her the chance to hone her acting skills, and clear out her sinuses at the same time.

Although usually very intelligent, her offhanded attitude toward life will leave you wondering whether all her synapses are firing in sequence. She will forget to balance the checkbook for months, coast into the gas station on a fume and a prayer, and swear that the refrigerator was full just yesterday. If you intend to have a decent retirement income and eat regularly, you will have to control the purse strings and learn how to cook.

No other woman in the Universe comes on so devoted, self-less, and understanding, and departs with a bigger chunk of your bloody heart stuck on her little pink fingernails. And she will be fluttering those artistic hands long after you've run screaming for the nearest therapist's couch.

If You Are One-Born Rotten

I don't know, I don't care, and it doesn't make any difference.

JACK KEROUAC (MARCH 12)

Pisces has often been called the *dustbin* of the zodiac. *Mental hospital* is a closer description. On your trek around the karmic wheel, you've not only picked up everyone else's bad habits, you've managed to forgo most of the good ones.

You are as obtuse as Taurus, anal as Virgo, and as wishy-washy as Libra. You blather as much as Gemini and Sagittarius put together, but your conversation is limited to instant replays of all the boring details of your crises-laden life. When you want something you can knock down more little old ladies than an Aries fighting to be first at a Macy's white sale. You are as freaked-out as Aquarius, obsessed as Scorpio, and whiny as a Cancer with a sore throat. Your penchant for theatrics makes the most flamboyant Leo look reticent, and your opinion of yourself is higher than that of a Capricorn who's just fore-closed on a Swiss bank.

You also have the special-to-you-alone gift for viewing life from a perpetually unworkable slant. You are so afraid of con-flict that you would rather eat worms than confront a prob-lem. But that's fine with you because it gives you the excuse to lie on the couch all day, flipping the remote and sighing.

The cliché of the lights are on but no one's home was no doubt first used to describe a Fish. You will fade out in the middle of commuter traffic going seventy, wake up in the next town, and have absolutely no idea how you got there.

Every Pisces is addicted to something. The obvious dangers are booze and drugs. However, serial romances, food, TV and excessive sleep are also ways you avoid dealing with reality. You are probably a lifetime member of every organization with *Anonymous* in the title.

Pisces have every psychological and psychosomatic illness known to man and participate in medical research trials more often than any other sign. You love the attention and use the twenty-five dollars to buy wine. You are so afraid of confrontation that trying to carry on a conversation with you is like talking to a bobble-head doll. You can't make a decision, no matter how inconsequential, and have the social presence of a door-mat. But, you do hate to see suffering. That's why you wear dark glasses.

Your favorite TV shows are the *Jerry Lewis Telethon* and the *PTL Club*. You love to cry along with fellow Fish Jerry, and to self-righteously bash those lacquer-haired televangelists.

As the last sign of the zodiac, you've walked in every other sign's shoes at least once. And slept in all their beds. You charm the pants off anyone—literally. However, you are so reality-challenged that you don't want a life, you want a movie.

Pisces make good actors, faith healers, vice cops, savants, and drag queens. You are also psychic; however you are so self-absorbed that the only future you care about is your own.

You don't do realism. Instead you prefer to view life from either your internal set of rose-colored glasses, or from a state of altered consciousness. Either way, you drift through the years with your head in the sand, preferring your fantasies and dragging behind you an endless line of losers you call family and friends. But that's OK with you, since it gives you an excuse to drink and bitch.

You are the chameleon of the Universe, and the shades of every other sign flutter through your soul. Because you are so acquiescent and hate conflict, you are invariably underestimated. Once you learn to quit underestimating yourself, that quality is precisely what will give you the edge over every other sign.

You can quiet an Aries temper tantrum with one icy look, and yawn in the face of Sagittarius' bellicose belching. You can steal the spotlight from any Leo and roar louder when you don't get your way. Earth signs are easily subdued. Raging Bull will soon find himself in the barn with a nose-ring. Virgo and Capricorn are much too solid, and you dispatch these odd ducks, calculators and all, to the outer limits of your awareness. Air signs Aquarius, Gemini, and Libra's petulant barbs scatter over your calm nature. You and the other Water signs, Cancer and Scorpio, understand each other on a soul level and, therefore, rarely have serious confrontations.

Yours is the philosophy of "Live and let live." Let other people scramble to grab the spotlight, run the world, or claw their way to the top; you are too busy making your dreams come true, quietly and determinedly behind the scenes. Years from now when all those people who underestimated you are taking sitz baths in the old folks' home, you can send them a picture of yourself soaking up the sun on a beach in the South Seas.

It's ALL Relative—The Pisces Family

> *You have brains in your head. You have feet in your shoes. You can steer yourself, any direction you choose. You're on your own.*
> Dr. Seuss (Theodor Geisel, March 2)

Being in a Pisces family is like watching The Brady Bunch meet Freddie Krueger. The resident Fish think they are the Bradys, but you will feel like you are wandering along Elm Street.

Pisces parents mean well, but vacillate between being overprotective and so permissive that you end up calling from jail for bail money. Of course, they will blame themselves for letting you out of the house in the first place, but it won't help much when you are eating your meals through the doggie door because they've locked you in the garage until graduation.

Fish parents cause more children to run away from home than all others combined. This is because they have the worst traits of every other sign. They dole out as meager an allowance as a Virgo, bark orders with the precision of a Leo drilling you on how to clean your room, and analyze every mood, decision, and look with the determination of a Gemini deciding whether or not you need therapy.

Mom will harangue you to avoid strangers, wear your coat, and eat your vegetables every day of your life. And Dad will teach you how to watch three TVs simultaneously. Both will drive you nuts with their endless procrastination.

If you want to go to the prom in April, you had better start prodding your mom to take you shopping in August. That way with her endless appointments, classes, visits to the sick, and tryouts for the latest local play, she will be able to pencil you in on her calendar by March 15.

You can forget Dad altogether, unless he's in one of his rare bursts of boundless energy; then expect to rush through a year's worth of errands all at once. Pisces parents are either in "on" or "off" mode when it comes to parental responsibility and, secretly, they wish you could grow up on your own.

Pisces babies sleep soundly, eat heartily, and are generally good-natured. However, your little Fish does all these things by his or her own inner clock, versus real-world time. As a toddler, they exist on a different plane and live in a private world of fantasy. Provide plenty of paper, crayons, and Dr. Seuss books to complement their active imaginations.

Pisces teens discover the angst of puppy love at an early age and spend hours writing in their diaries, or moping about their latest crush. They also have a tendency to avoid responsibility, cry over every small slight, and forgo their homework in favor of watching a favorite movie. Helping yours to confront small issues now will prepare him or her to deal with bigger issues as an adult. Boost their self-confidence every chance you get and never make fun of this kid's dreams.

Fish-head brothers and sisters spend most of their time in front of their mirrors practicing an acceptance speech. Whether it's for an Academy Award or Teacher of the Year is irrelevant, as each dreams of someday being one of the rich and famous. They are moody, and may laugh one minute and yell at you the next. They are usually harmless, but frequently so spacey that they lock themselves in the bedroom and listen to loud music all day. If this is your room too, make sure you have your own key and buy him or her a set of headphones.

Surviving a family of Fish is easy once you understand that they are all susceptible to the power of suggestion. With a little foresight and planning you can not only have your way, but also that new sound system you want for your birthday.

Office Party—Bitches, Snitches, and the Chronically Inert

We don't see things as they are. We see things as we are.
Anaïs Nin (February 21)

The only thing rarer than a Fish at the top of a corporate ladder is twenty-dollar steak. To a Pisces, sitting in an office all day, every day, doing the same thing day in and day out is cruel and unusual punishment. Besides, most corporations frown on the three-martini lunch. If you do have a Pisces boss, you will probably see him or her only a couple of days a month. The rest of the time Boss Fish will be on the road and you will be happily left on your own.

Fish can spout orders and occasionally will snap off a brittle remark about how you screwed up that last advertising deal, but most of the time he or she will spend the mornings making plans for lunch. After lunch, you can forget it. Fill a Pisces with rich food and a couple of drinks, and he will either take the rest of the day off, or come back, lock his office door under the guise of catching up on the pile on his desk, and sleep the afternoon away.

Not only do your Pisces' coworkers not want your job, they don't want theirs. Pisces are too busy dreaming of running away to the nearest tropical island or mooning over their latest love disaster. Instead of trying to usurp your position in any business situation, Pisces prefers to sit around and bitch about how much better he or she could do it. Either sex will seldom make an actual move on your desk.

Gaslight one by calling her bluff. Simply offer to switch positions. You'll find yourself on the receiving end of a vacant stare followed by some unintelligible mumbling as she hurries back to her own cubicle. Don't worry about her trying to get even. She may bitch and moan, but will be so upset at having her bluff called she'll forget about wanting your job.

Can't We All Get Along?

Wondering how to live happily ever after with such a tortured and demented soul? With a little practice, you can tell the dolphins from the sharks every time.

Shark Attacks

Fishes of both sexes and all ages share a genuine need for periods of solitude. This is how an ultra-sensitive Pisces copes. In addition to reacting to the everyday anxiety of their personal lives, they also sense emotions and read undercurrents that run through the general atmosphere. When stressed and tired, they get brusque, short-tempered, and fussy. That's your cue to take them out for a quiet dinner in the farthest corner of the darkest restaurant you can find. Then take them home and tuck them into bed with a good book or meditation tape.

Depressed Fish

Everyone thinks Fish are so far off in la-la land that nothing penetrates their fantasy world to bother them. This is the furthest thing from the truth. Pisces are the best listeners in the Universe and tend to get deeply involved in the problems of friends and family. Conversely, they also believe that they should depend on no one but themselves to get where they want to go, which makes them very reluctant to ask for help, especially when they are desperate and floundering.

When a Fish's sensory system is overloaded you will find them either sleeping too much or lying on the couch, listlessly flipping the remote. That's your cue to tell them they can depend on you for anything while you brew a pot of herbal tea and light a sandalwood candle. Then gather them up in a bear hug and start listening.

Bottle Bluefish

Substance abuse, or overindulgence of any kind, is a very real danger to Pisces of both sexes. Fish are the rescuers of the zodiac. They often have a profound compassion and empathy for the human condition, and feel guilty that they personally can't help other people change. Too often, drugs or alcohol dull their senses so the Fish can mold fact into a less-abrasive version of reality.

If your Fish is habitually drinking, overeating, or sleeping twenty hours a day, you can safely bet it's because he or she is unhappy about something that they don't want to face. Whether it's family, job, or their relationship with you, the kindest thing for you to do is to take them to the beach, sans any chocolate or other mood-altering substances, and gently, but firmly, make them talk it out.

Floundering Fish

Rarely will a Fish get fired from a job. More often, they float from one menial position to another in a series of repetitive failures. This isn't because they are either stupid, or lazy. It's because they are trying to fit the world's definition of what they should be. Fish are destined to create. Whether yours secretly wants to design costumes, or teach piano, your job is to support his or her dream.

They need to sleep, eat, and work at their own pace and rhythm. Give yours your unconditional support and help restructure the household routine, and you'll soon find yourself living, if not in the lap of luxury, then at the very least in the home of harmony.

Quick Tips for Emergencies

)(Pisces need private time.

)(When real life gets too hard, take them to a movie, an antique mall, or the nearest body of water.

)(Remember romance.

)(Praise them frequently.

)(Gaslight them by calling their bluff.

Sharks and Little Fishes

Joey Buttafuoco
John Wayne Gacy
Patty Hearst
Brian "Kato" Kaelin
Ted Kennedy
"Night Stalker" Richard Ramirez
Mr. Rogers
Bugsy Siegel
Dorothy Stratton
Darryl Strawberry